Augustus Gurney

The Home Life of Jesus of Nazareth

And other Sermons

Augustus Gurney

The Home Life of Jesus of Nazareth
And other Sermons

ISBN/EAN: 9783744742375

Printed in Europe, USA, Canada, Australia, Japan

Cover: Foto ©Lupo / pixelio.de

More available books at **www.hansebooks.com**

THE HOME LIFE

OF

JESUS OF NAZARETH

&c.

BY THE
REV. AUGUSTUS GURNEY, M.A.
VICAR OF WRIBBENHALL, KIDDERMINSTER, IN THE DIOCESE OF WORCESTER

RIVINGTONS
London, Oxford, and Cambridge
1871

CONTENTS.

The Home Life of Jesus of Nazareth.
(EPIPHANY.)

	PAGE
INTRODUCTION	1
I. THE GREAT NAZARENE	5
II. THE JOY OF JOSEPH AND OF MARY . .	19
III. THE CHILD JESUS IN THE TEMPLE .	33
IV. THE COMING UNTO A PERFECT MAN .	45
V. GROWTH IN QUIETNESS	61
VI. OUR LORD BELOVED OF MEN . . .	75
VII. THE FATHER'S SANCTION OF THE SON'S HOME LIFE	89

The Temptations.
(LENT.)

INTRODUCTION . . .	105
I. THE FIRST TEMPTATION . .	107
II. THE SECOND TEMPTATION . . .	121
III. THE THIRD TEMPTATION . . .	135

The Obedience unto Death.

(LENT.)

		PAGE
INTRODUCTION	. . . .	153
I. THE FATHER'S LOVE	. . . . .	155
II. THE ATONEMENT	. . . . .	171
III. SELF-SURRENDER	. .	189

The Home Life of Jesus of Nazareth.

"Is not this the carpenter, the son of Mary?"

INTRODUCTION.

MANY thoughts arise on the mention of Nazareth, of Nazareth where Jesus was "brought up." Yet how little do we know concerning the wonderful events transacted there, we who would gladly know so much. How shall Christians penetrate the mysteries of Nazareth,—that village or mountain-town, and yet city in Scripture phraseology,—difficult of access in all senses, the place itself remote, set in a hollow on a mountain side? We may indeed visit the modern town of Nazareth at this present time, and happy are they who can do so. Men can even drink at will from the very fountain, it may be, at which Mary filled her pitcher. But how conjure Nazareth back to the eye of faith as it appeared when inhabited by the Saviour of the world? How perceive Him, the Saviour, the Messias yet unrevealed, labouring in the workshop, or conversing with His mother and foster-father, or studying the law and the prophets, or frequenting the synagogue "as His custom was" on the Sabbath-day, or holding commune with His Heavenly Father, or engaged in kindly intercourse with kinsfolk and neighbours, so conciliating their good-will, or possibly even in earlier years mingling in the pastimes of youthful companions?

There will be much indeed to learn in heaven, much that is delightful, of the Saviour's home life in Nazareth, of His priceless words and heavenly ways. But are there no earthly records that we may consult meanwhile? May we, for instance, have recourse—if not for facts yet for some faint suggestive hints—to what are called the Apocryphal Gospels, written professedly to throw light on our Lord's youth and childhood? No, surely not; those spurious gospels are really barren and dark, born of childish inanity, and, worse, of actual falsehood. We turn from them with a just indignation. Rather than consult these, we may well be content to await Heaven's own blest light. But again I ask, Are there no true, no inspired sources of information to which we may turn already? Yes, God be praised, such sources exist for our abiding wonder and delight. First, there are the glorious Gospel intimations concerning the home life of Jesus, sweet if not full, precious and inexhaustible if rare. And then, there exist the writings of the prophets. Whoso shall scan these last with reverent eye to see if, by their means, some little supplementary light may not be shed upon that home period of deep humility, shall not go wholly unrewarded. And may we not bring to our aid also our knowledge of the Saviour's later ways, and thence draw lawful inferences? All this, doubtless, we may do without incurring blame. And yet little, very little, will have been accomplished after all to bridge over the chasm in our Lord's history which parts His early childhood from His manhood.

But, nevertheless, may these faint far-off glimpses of our Saviour's home life, drawn exclusively from the records of Holy Scripture, serve as profitable subjects for the meditation of Christians. And even by this artless endeavour to realize and to open out that which has been revealed, may something of a more fresh and living interest attach in our eyes (if that be possible) to the Saviour's after deeds and words. So let Him come at least before us when He enters on His public ministry, as no stranger, but as Jesus of Nazareth of a truth.

The several subjects that follow are treated with simplicity, and the issues aimed at are practical; but it is true that the highest questions are raised from time to time, forasmuch as he who considers thoughtfully any period of the life of the Lord Jesus on earth must needs be brought face to face with mighty mysteries. Chiefest of the mysteries that confront us here is that of the Twofold Nature in One Person. And whereas in former ages Christian men have contended more especially for the Divinity of our Master, and have won countless victories of the faith in honour of the Godhead, it would seem to be rather reserved for believers in these latter days to discern, with more and more of fulness and of adoring wonder, the Man within the God.

I.
THE GREAT NAZARENE.

THE GREAT NAZARENE.

S. Matthew ii. 23.

"*And he (Joseph) came and dwelt in a city called Nazareth: that it might be fulfilled which was spoken by the prophets, He (Jesus) shall be called a Nazarene.*"

THE Holy Family had fled into Egypt to avoid the persecution of King Herod. On their return to their own country, Nazareth presented itself as a safe haven; and thither Joseph led the young Child and His mother, not without divine guidance. In this choice of abode there was every way a fitness. For not only was Nazareth, the mountain-town or city, from its very remoteness, eminently adapted for the bringing up in retirement of the Messiah; but further, it had been the former home of Mary and of Joseph. There, it would seem, Joseph had followed his occupation of a carpenter; there, it is likely, he owned house and workshed and land, on however humble a scale. And there chiefly were to be found such friends and relatives as Joseph and Mary were possessed of. Consequently no place would hold out more numerous attractions or better means of subsistence to the Holy Family than Nazareth, whilst incidentally, by its selection, all remote and seemingly forgotten corners of God's earth, and their inhabitants, may be said to have received honour, and to have been proved to be partakers of His special love and care.

But that is not all, brethren. Nazareth was chosen to be the Saviour's place of abode, so St. Matthew tells us in the text, "that it might be fulfilled which was spoken by the prophets, He shall be called a Nazarene." Now, it is quite true that St. Matthew need not be held to cite here so much any particular prophet as all: "that it might be fulfilled which was spoken by the prophets." And all the prophets may be said to have set forth the abject, lowly condition of Messiah, so pointing forward in a manner to the Divine Dweller in despised Nazareth, so by implication saying of Him, "He shall be called a Nazarene." And yet may one particular prophecy seem to have been more especially in St. Matthew's mind, even that which is contained in the Book of Judges (xii. 5), and which has a primary allusion to Samson: "The child shall be a

Nazarite." " Nazarene " and " Nazarite " are indeed scarcely convertible terms, yet do they bear much affinity to one another : and if, as is most certain, our Blessed Lord was both a Nazarene and a Nazarite, then perhaps we need not hesitate to apply to Him, for purposes of edification, both passages alike.

The Child of Nazareth was of necessity a Nazarene. And none, I think, will be found to deny that Jesus, like Samson and like John the Baptist, was a Nazarite in the spiritual sense of being set apart for God's service from the womb.

But would you know, brethren, what a Nazarite, more strictly speaking, was? A Nazarite, then, was not necessarily a dweller in Nazareth, but was any Jewish man or Jewish woman dwelling any where and set apart by a vow to God's service for a shorter or a longer time, as the case might be. We read first of the Nazarites (not of the dwellers in Nazareth, but of the religious persons so-called) in the 6th chapter of the Book of Numbers : " When either man or woman shall separate themselves to vow a vow of a Nazarite, to separate themselves unto the Lord "—then (and here I condense the actual words) they shall separate themselves from wine and strong drink, from the use of the razor, and from the touching of any dead body.

Such were the ceremonial rules of the ancient Nazarites. But the Lord Jesus, as we know, did not think fit to conform to those ceremonial regulations. It is likely indeed, or at least it is possible, that no razor ever came upon His sacred head; but whereas the Nazarites neither drank wine nor touched any dead body, He, as we know, did both. He even turned water into wine at a marriage-feast, and He took by the hand the daughter of Jairus after she was dead, when her spirit came again. And in like manner the followers of the Lord Jesus also, so far from not touching any dead body, are forward in showing to their dead the last offices of affection, with no shrinking from actual contact with the lifeless clay. But although those ceremonial observances were not for Him or for His, the Lord Jesus, we cannot doubt, soared immeasurably above all others who at any time bore the religious name of Nazarite, in respect of that surpassing holiness, that being set apart peculiarly to God's service, which constituted the essence of the title; He was indeed the Great Nazarite, or crowning glory of all Nazarites.

But it is time, brethren, to leave on one side explanation, and to enter somewhat more closely on our sacred theme, even that of the Saviour's home life in

Nazareth. Let us then, so to speak, bare-headed, and with lowly adoring hearts, draw nigh to our sacred Master in the chosen place of His retirement.

The home life of Jesus in Nazareth is not altogether hidden from our view. The prophet Isaiah and the Evangelist St. Luke more especially, have each, in no small measure, as we may see hereafter, cast the light of inspiration on the period which elapsed between the Saviour's birth and His showing to Israel. True indeed it is that very much remains untold, and that therefore the term "hidden life" is here not out of place; but enough has been revealed by the Holy Spirit for Christian instruction and delight, enough also to justify the use of that nearer and dearer term, the home life of Jesus.

And, as I think, we may store our minds not only with images of sweetness, but with the holiest of examples, even from the consideration of those simple words of the text, "He shall be called a Nazarene," supplemented by those other words from the Book of Judges, "the child shall be a Nazarite." For He who was the Great Nazarene has struck out a far more lofty ideal of holiness than that of the ceremonial Nazarite. The Lord Jesus, as we all know, beloved brethren, led in Nazareth a life of poverty, chastity, and obedience,

—herein, in these three great particulars, setting an example of personal holiness, never to be surpassed, to all who at any time should call upon His name. The Lord Jesus, by His home life in Nazareth, set an example of holiness to the ordinary Christian, yea, even to the very last and least among ourselves. Truly, beloved, we cannot discern here so-called counsels of perfection intended only for such as exceptionally forsake all for their Master's sake in obedience to some extraordinary call, but we must see rather plainest duties for all Christian men. That is nothing less than a universal lesson which is to be drawn from the example given by our Master Christ in Nazareth.

And now to say a little under the three heads of poverty, chastity, obedience.

The great Nazarene was poor: not indeed poor, so far as we can judge, like the beggar who has only a crust between himself and starvation, but rather poor with that decent and seemly poverty, which, by God's appointment, falls to the lot of earth's working millions, who having food and raiment are therewith content. It is our Master who has said—and His life on earth has but lent a fuller meaning to His words—"A man's life consisteth not in the abundance of the things which he possesseth." And it is certain that family affection and true refinement can and do exist among the godly poor. That which makes too many a lowly lot distressing, and almost unendurable, is not the absence of wealth, and of the pleasures and luxuries which wealth brings with it; but *is* coarseness, ignorance, brutality, disorder, drunkenness, blasphemy, in a word, forgetfulness of God. These are the things which defile the home life of too many a working man's family. I speak of those who amid the ranks of labour should of right occupy a decent, a comely, an honourable position, like in kind to that of Jesus of Nazareth. For who can doubt that the home of Jesus, however simple and poor it may have been, was refined above all earth's palaces in those things which bring real refinement, namely, in affection, in sweet temper, in heart knowledge, in fair order, and in godliness? Again and again, beloved, when we would fain pity the Lord Jesus for the life of poverty and of simplicity which He willingly endured, we shall, I believe, find ourselves unable so to do; nay more, we may even be overcome by a feeling of shame. For when once we have considered that He was Very God of Very God, who led a man's life upon earth, the question of a little more or a little less of well-being in the worldly circumstances of the Messiah sinks into insignificance. At least, and herein let us all rejoice, the Lord Jesus was sheltered in Nazareth by the pure and the true, by the blessed Virgin and by Joseph. And, as our hearts assure us, that was a better, happier home, that was a nobler and a more exalted home, which the Redeemer found in Nazareth, than falls to the lot of many an envied youth and maiden lapped in prosperity. " Jesus increased in favour with God and man." What more would we have? Wealth is *not* of that paramount importance which we are apt to attach to it. And the Saviour's willing poverty not only endears Him to our hearts, but may be said to constitute a Divine protest to that effect. You, my brethren, that have to work hard for your daily bread, do you hear these things, and can you rest unmoved? Surely, of all great classes, working men should be the very first and foremost to welcome that mighty Saviour who deigned to share their lot! Would that each working man might aim at making his home like to the home of Jesus of Nazareth. Would indeed that all of us in every condition of life might strive to attain to this true pattern, to this highest ideal of what home life should be. And, in particular, let all, poor and rich alike, seek to be poor or lowly in spirit, loving and loveworthy.

But next, the Great Nazarene was pure, was chaste. Yes, purity white as the driven snow was part of the hidden life of Jesus. Joseph, Jacob's son, who endured a fiery trial in Egypt, is to us but a faint and feeble type of the perfect purity of our Lord and Master. The spotlessness of the lily, the blue depths of the sky, the innocence of the child, are all but superficial types of the measureless purity which was enshrined in Jesus of Nazareth. No life, dear brethren, can be altogether unhappy which is pure. Purity is the crowning excellency of life. Let all go, we might well say, so that that be kept! It is that which makes life lovely if we have it, unlovely if we have it not, and in the long run painful to ourselves. But to enlarge on purity in connexion with our Divine Master would indeed be presumptuous, so I forbear, and pass on. How shall impure lips speak on so high, so glorious, so marvellous a theme? Only let me repeat distinctly that the home or hidden life of Jesus of Nazareth holds out to us an example of absolute purity of mind, body, and spirit, and so enforces on us the necessity of the longing, the aim, after purity in thought and will.

But once more, the Great Nazarene was obedient. He was subject to His earthly parents until, on attaining to full manhood, He claimed justly to act for Himself, and show Himself to the world in an hour of His own choice; yet even then He yielded gracefully to a mother's barely suggested desire. We see that the Lord's obedience to His earthly mother had a limit. But He was subject in all things to His Heavenly Father's will, yea, in *all* things, and to the end. See, then, in Jesus of Nazareth, dearly beloved, the great example of obedience to parents and to all who are placed in authority over us. But see in Jesus, your beloved Lord, above all, the great example of obedience to our Heavenly Father's will, and seek with Him to be obedient from the cradle to the grave.

Thus has it been in some sort shown to you, my brethren, that the Great Nazarene was most holy in aim and deed, holier than all who were called Nazarites because they had separated themselves by a vow to God's service. Yes, He was infinitely holier than these all by reason of His willing poverty, chastity, and true obedience. Yet, be it noted that the Saviour never severed or separated Himself from the common duties of mankind. Rather did He dwell in the world and leaven it by His sacred influence. And surely we may not unfitly say, "the disciple is not above his Master, nor the servant above his Lord. It is enough for the disciple that he be as his Master, and the servant as his Lord." So much is certain, without the taking of any special or extraordinary obligations, there are high and noble duties—ay, none higher, none more noble—incumbent on the lowly Christian. For one vow we have already taken, even our baptismal vow, which includes all others; namely, to renounce all sins, to believe in God, and to serve Him. And by this vow we are called to lead a hidden life to the Lord, a life of poverty of spirit, of true chastity or purity of heart—whether in or out of married life—and of honest obedience. Yea, by this vow we are called to be Nazarites in a true and lofty Christian sense; we are set apart as men and women whose lives are dedicated to God, even whilst we dwell and labour among men, children of the kingdom of heaven though dwellers upon earth, and dwellers, as we humbly hope, hereafter, for Christ's sake, in a city with everlasting "foundations, whose builder and maker is God."

II.
THE JOY OF JOSEPH AND OF MARY.

THE JOY OF JOSEPH AND OF MARY.

St. Luke ii. 33.

"And Joseph and His mother marvelled at those things which were spoken of Him."

TO us the full deep meaning of the mystery of all the ages, the Incarnation of the Son of God, is revealed; but it is plain that this was not apprehended by Joseph and Mary, no, nor was meant so to be. And the wisdom of this arrangement is not far to seek. The knowledge of our Lord's earthly parents was doubtless incomplete in mercy, lest excess of awe and delight should overpower them, lest also they should be hindered from exercising parental authority over the Holy Child Jesus: for how should they give commands to Him whom they had once recognized as God Incarnate? And then Christ would not have been as one of us, trained up in obedience to earthly authority, would not have been as the heir, who, though Lord of all, was to be under tutors and governors until the time appointed of the Father. But so much at least Joseph and Mary must have seen: this Babe committed to their care was in some sense of God. Many circumstances combined to raise their wonder, as—the song of the angels, the adoration of the shepherds and of the wise men, the prophecies of Elizabeth and Zacharias, of Simeon and of Anna, and first and foremost the message of the angel Gabriel; and so, as we read in the text, "Joseph and His mother marvelled at those things which were spoken of Him." Joseph was, as we all know, but a carpenter, though of the royal line of David; and Mary, who was of like royal descent, appears to have been in a no more exalted station of life than her husband. It would be impossible to treat of the home life of the Lord Jesus in Nazareth without making particular mention of His earthly parents. So then let me speak of them briefly in the order in which Holy Scripture brings them before us.

Joseph is described as "a just man." That surely means not only that he was considerate in respect of not being minded to make his wife a public example, but further that he was a man to be relied upon in life,—a worthy, honest, truthful man, a man to be trusted both by God and man. Oh, what honour, what amazing honour, is here bestowed by the Almighty on so-called justice or honesty, when that is the one only quality which is plainly attributed to Joseph in the Word of God! Joseph does not appear to have been remarkable for any thing besides. Not so much as one single word that he spoke has been recorded. But he was "a just man," and that is enough to account for God's favour towards him. That is enough to account for the immense dignity bestowed upon him by the Almighty, that of being foster-father to the Lord Jesus. Ah see, brethren, who they are that are trusted and favoured by God; not the learned, not the polished, not even such as are remarkable merely for their devotion, but the honest and the true. He who has come down to us and will go down to remotest posterity as the revered head and chief of the Holy Family, as the protector and possible instructor of the Lord's childhood and boyhood, was before all things an honest man. So let the lesson sink deep into our hearts. So let truth and honesty be endeared to us, be ennobled in our sight. Joseph was "a just man." Be sure that he was faithful to his trust. When danger threatened the Holy Child from King Herod, he shrank not from protecting the Infant Christ and His mother on their flight into Egypt.

When the Virgin presented her Son in the Temple, Joseph was present. And later, when our Redeemer was lost for three days at the age of twelve, and after that was found sitting with the doctors, Joseph and Mary still sought for Him together. Our Lord was subject to Joseph as He was to Mary, for so the Word of God assures us. When Joseph died is not known, but it is supposed that he died in a good old age long before our Lord entered on His public ministry. And in the natural course of events the tears of the Lord Jesus must have fallen beside His foster-father's tomb.

The blessed Virgin's character next claims consideration at our hands. We are apt, my dear brethren, to dwell less than we ought to dwell on the beauty of her character and on the wondrous honour bestowed upon her person, as stated in the Holy Scriptures, because, alas! multitudes of misguided Christians pay to her that secondary worship which, as we are firmly persuaded, is absolutely forbidden and unlawful. But we, who by God's grace are resolved to yield our trust, our confidence, our love, to God, "the jealous God," rather than to the dearest and best of His creatures, who purpose from our very souls to worship and call upon God only,—we, I say, ought not to allow any blind terror of excess to mislead us in this matter, to narrow our hearts and understandings. We need not shrink from recognizing and proclaiming all the blessed Virgin's purity, love, and meekness. How pure must she not have been who was chosen to be the Redeemer's earthly mother! How sweet and lowly is not her converse with the angel Gabriel, ending with the words, " Behold the handmaid of the Lord ; be it unto me according to thy word "! What a faithful, trusting, noble spirit is shown in the *Magnificat*, or the Song of the blessed Virgin Mary, which we recite in the order of our evening prayer! What a reverent, thoughtful disposition is implied in the words, " But Mary kept all these things, and pondered them in her heart "! How little does she seem to have thought of herself on any occasion, fixing indeed all her thoughts on her divine Son ! Until her Son was thirty years of age, and probably long after the death of Joseph, the Virgin lived with the Lord Jesus in Nazareth, rather protected, humanly speaking, by her Son, than acting in any sense as His protectress. It was not granted to Mary to precede her Son in death ; but, as we know, it was her bitter lot to behold Him crucified. The brief years of our Lord's public ministry may well have proved to her years of overwhelming anxiety, years wherein, from apprehension of His death long before that death ensued,

Simeon's prophecy would already be fulfilled in part, "Yea, a sword shall pierce through thy own soul also." Yet must even those years of supreme anxiety have been also years of loving pride and exultation in her Son's courage and His surpassing greatness. For how should the Virgin Mary have proved an exception to all good and noble mothers, who, as we know, even when they most dread the consequences of their sons' heroic conduct, yet glory therein? And to end this brief mention of the blessed Virgin's excellencies, she never gave but one command recorded in God's holy Word, and that was, "Whatsoever He saith unto you, do it."

And now to speak briefly of Joseph and of Mary together, and of their companionship with and their tender relationship to the Lord of life. It is to be doubted, my dear brethren, whether we at all realize the thought of their great happiness. Yet to a thoughtful Christian mind it may surely seem that that happiness must have been well-nigh complete. To go in and out with Jesus daily, and to call Him Son, must it not have been delight unalloyed, save by the possible fear of what was yet to come? To consult with Him in the affairs of daily life, to speak with Him of heaven, to hear Him read, at times, it may be, the prophecies that bore upon His own birth and life and death—although one and all imperfectly discerned by them—must it not have been a pure and exquisite delight? To meet His gentle looks, to watch His wise and loving ways, to mark His earnest communion with His Heavenly Father; must not all this have constituted the extreme of mortal happiness? True, they knew not fully who He was; but the light of heaven shone in His eyes, and would be felt deep within their hearts. And this at least they knew for certain, that He, their Son and Foster-son, He the mysterious boon from heaven, was to be a benefactor of the human race, was in some sense to "save His people from their sins." Again, I ask, was there ever happiness on earth to equal that of Joseph and of Mary? And in that happiness I humbly conceive that our Lord had His perfect human part, a fact apt to be undiscerned by many loving Christians, who seem to me too anxious to dwell exclusively on our Blessed Master's humiliations, touching lightly on the secret compensations of purest human affection as well as delight in the working out of His Heavenly Father's will.

And now, beloved, the question, the practical question for us will arise, How far have we a share in this very happiness? Some of you perhaps may be disposed to reply, "The joy of Joseph, and of Mary (and yet more of the Holy Child) was a joy apart, a joy with which we can have nothing in common, save at the utmost by distant sympathy, for we are not closely related to the Lord as were they; He is not our Son, neither are any of us His mother or His foster-father. We dwell not in that beloved close circle, we are not sharers of His home."

Nay, beloved, we may not say so; we ought not to be thus ready to disclaim relationship with the Son of Man. For do but call to mind the Lord's own words, when, looking round about on them which sat about Him, He said, " Behold My mother and My brethren! For whosoever shall do the will of God, the same is My brother, and My sister, and mother." So then, incredible as it may sound, we ought to stand at this moment in one or other of these near relationships to the Lord Jesus. If we "do the will of God:" that is the condition laid down by the Lord Himself; if we endeavour, by the Holy Spirit's aid, to be honest, faithful, manly and true like Joseph; if we seek to be pure and meek and loving and trustful like the blessed Virgin! And it is likely that I am speaking even now to some whom our Lord would not have scorned to call "mother," "sister," "brethren:" so then, mothers of Christ, sisters and brethren of Christ, do not disown your relationship to your Redeemer—that be far from you; but rather, by "doing His will," seek to draw that relationship ever closer. And, in particular, let the love which reigned between the dwellers in the carpenter's house in Nazareth reign between ourselves and our earthly relatives, reign between husband and wife, between parents and children, and also between brothers and sisters. Every family should be a holy family, bearing affinity and possessing likeness to that holiest of all families upon the face of the earth which dwelt in Nazareth.

Thus, then, it *is* in our power to claim Christ for our own. And if the peculiar joy of Joseph and Mary can never be ours,—that of watching (all unconsciously though it were) the human growth of the Lord of all, and hearing His sweet voice about the house, and following His every movement with our eyes—yet in heaven hereafter there await us even greater joys than these in the conscious constant vision of our Lord in glory. And meanwhile already here on earth we may delight in Him as much as did His earthly parents in Nazareth. For if Mary and Joseph gathered treasures of grace and wisdom from the lips of the youthful Lord, these we may gather no less from the lips of the same Lord when come to man's estate, and almost I had said in a higher degree than they. For if only the will be not wanting to us, we can take delight in those miracles of mercy and of power, and in that obedience unto death, of which Joseph at the least, whilst he abode on earth, knew nothing. If only the will be not wanting to us, we can go in and out with Jesus in our lives, dwell in His presence, be made one with Him in His sacraments, glory in His courage and in His greatness, mourn with Him in His sufferings, and triumph with Him in His victories. And we can adore Him as God, Him whom even the blessed Virgin, before He was risen from the dead, understood rather to be sent from God than to be Very God of Very God. Understand then once for all, beloved, how mighty are our privileges. Did not our Lord say concerning one unsurpassed by any born of women, even John the Baptist, "He that is least in the kingdom of heaven is greater than he?" What need we wonder then that our privileges as Christians—our privileges not our attainments—should be even greater than were those of Joseph and Mary in Nazareth? And now I ask again, May we not learn to love the Saviour as dearly as His earthly parents loved Him? Ay, truly, if only the will be not wanting to us! We are brought wonderfully near to our Master. We may dwell with Him and He with us. "According to our faith shall it be unto us." This is God's own word, and it contains a very depth of truth and wonder. "According to our faith shall it be unto us." "Lord, increase our faith!"

III.
THE CHILD JESUS IN THE TEMPLE.

THE CHILD JESUS IN THE TEMPLE.

St. Luke ii. part of ver. 49.
"*Wist ye not that I must be about My Father's business?*"

DURING the prolonged, and, for the more part, hidden period of the home life of the Lord Jesus in Nazareth, one, and one only event stands out clearly revealed to us in broad and bold relief. We shall scarcely err, then, if to it we attribute a very singular degree of importance. That event (needs it to be said?) is the going up of the Holy Child to Jerusalem. The general reticence of the Scriptures with respect to the incidents of our Lord's childhood and youth is here for once strikingly broken. Here is one silvery harmonious peal rung upon bells that else are almost altogether silent; here is one rose allowed to waft its perfume from a secluded garden of roses; here is one star suffered to shine through the clouded vault of heaven.

The whole brief narrative before us is full of inexhaustible freshness and beauty, yielding, beneath the Holy Spirit's guidance, matter for undying wonder and adoration to the Church of God. In the narrative we see the Child Jesus setting forth with Joseph and His mother to keep the Feast of the Passover at Jerusalem. At this time He was twelve years old—equivalent, it is computed, to nearly fifteen years of age in our more temperate climate, where plants and men alike ripen less quickly than in the glowing East. It should seem that not before the age of twelve did Jewish children accompany their parents to the feast. And our Master was not to differ in this respect from the youth of His nation. So then, for the first time, as we may consider, since in unconscious infancy He had been taken up in aged Simeon's arms, Jesus was going up into the Holy City and to the Temple. This first going up may well have constituted to all Jewish youths, dwellers in the country, an event of exceeding interest. What, then, must it not have been to the Holy Child? to the youthful, albeit, it may be, in some measure, as yet unconscious Messiah? Surely, nothing less than a cause for all but overwhelming joy. But we may not linger over this opening portion of the narrative. The little company which set forth from Nazareth consisted of "kinsfolk and acquaintances" (as how indeed should the inhabitants of a place so inconsiderable have failed to have been known to one another?) and reached Jerusalem in safety. There in Jerusalem they duly kept the feast, attending the beautiful and gorgeous ceremonies of the Temple worship. And after that they set forth on their homeward journey. There is no need to remind you, brethren, how at the close of the first day's journey the Child Jesus was missed, and how, after three days spent in anxious search, He was found by His parents in the Temple. It is strange that they did not find Him there before. But, as matter of fact, they would seem to have sought for Him at the first elsewhere, probably in the houses of friends at Jerusalem, and only to have gone to the house of God as a last resort. At length, in any case, they turned their steps in the right direction at the right hour. They entered the precincts of the glorious Temple, and there, in one of the many outer chambers it is likely, they found the Child Jesus " sitting in the midst of the doctors, both hearing them and asking them questions." Do we wonder where the Holy Child had been sheltered at night during those three days? Not improbably in the house of one of the principal Rabbis

—the same, perhaps (for all must needs be conjecture here), who may have called the doctors of the law together to introduce this remarkable Child to them.

Under such circumstances, then, did the parents of the Lord Jesus find Him who was the desire of their eyes—their own holy, affectionate, wise, obedient child—the mysterious gift to them from Heaven. They found Him sitting amid a circle of learned men, the chief teachers of the then Church of God. When these questioned Him, He made answer, and even asked questions in His turn, as though seeking for instruction at their hands. Very striking is the picture here presented to us. It would seem that the wisdom as well as the humility of the Child Jesus were such as to delight those venerable men. We can well believe that all who drew near to Jesus as a child would love Him.

The questions and replies which passed on this memorable occasion have not been recorded. We shall never learn on this side of the grave what words of beauty and of wisdom those were which were spoken by the lips of the Child Jesus. As I have said already, food for undying wonder is here ministered to the Church of God. Did the looked-for coming of the Messiah form one subject of deep conference? Who shall say? Did our Blessed Saviour already at this time seek to convey a juster and a truer idea of the expected Messiah to His nation's wisest sons? We cannot tell. Did the Child Jesus point the attention of the Jewish sages to many a grave and awful word of prophecy by them hitherto in part misapprehended? Did He even point to words predicting the rejection and the death of shame, as well as the ultimate victory and triumph of the Messiah? Again, I say, we cannot tell. Only this we dare affirm,—much that was very glorious must assuredly have passed out of the Boy Lord's mind into the minds and hearts of the more willing and receptive among His hearers. It would seem that for the time being the great doctors of the law were most strangely moved. It is written, "And all that heard Him were astonished at His understanding and answers."

When Joseph and Mary, not without amazement, found their missing treasure—found Him who, it is likely, had never pained them before, this is what happened: one of the twain, she who had the most sacred of rights—the right of a mother—pressed forward to claim her child, whilst Joseph, the foster father of our Lord, stood by in silence. The mother, full of delight and wonder, and yet it may be conceiving that something of the nature of a reproach was demanded of her by the occasion, said very tenderly, " Son, why hast Thou thus dealt with us ? behold, Thy father and I have sought Thee sorrowing." Might it not, in truth, appear from these words, " Thy father and I," as if up to this time the Holy Child had been led unresistingly to accord to Joseph the sacred title of father? But now (with no little delicacy) He was to place Himself, if only for a moment, on a right footing in respect of this matter. So then to His mother's words He answered, " How is it that ye sought Me ?"—meaning, it may be, hereby, How is it that ye sought Me with such anxiety, such alarm ? and again, far and wide all over Jerusalem ? and not rather with full trust and confidence have sought and found Me straightway here in the Temple of God? And then He continued in words of most mighty import, " Wist ye not that I must be about *My Father's* business?" or, as some prefer to render it (it makes no difference to the exceeding greatness of the saying), " Wist ye not that I must be in *My Father's* house?"

What a scene was here presented to the lookers on! to those Jewish Rabbis who would doubtless watch with curiosity and interest the meeting between the wonderful Child and His parents. Some of them may have trusted maliciously that the youth who had appealed so strongly to their faculty of wonder would be rated and gravely censured, whilst others with concern may have apprehended as much. But what did they see and hear? In the first place, all must have beheld the Virgin gazing on her recovered treasure with unutterable love; and next, all who heard the Heavenly Child's answer must at the least have acknowledged its mysterious dignity.

Let us hear that answer again, "Wist ye not that I must be about My Father's business?" or "in My Father's house?" That is the one revealed saying spoken by Jesus in the Temple at the age of twelve. Here truly is a peal of heavenly music which compensates for the long silence before and after. What matter that the words which passed between the Holy Child and the Rabbis should be as yet withheld, since this great word is given to us? In that mighty saying we behold the Holy Child claiming a son's relationship to the Almighty Father, even whilst He seeks lovingly to prepare His earthly parents for what the future should have in store for them of inevitable sorrows, partings, and regrets. As the Lord Jesus spoke these great recorded words, did His eyes kindle with heavenly light? Was Divinity suggested by His very aspect? It may be so; but for us it suffices that the words were spoken which satisfy all our hearts.

But pass we on to the end of the history. The Holy Child returned meekly and contentedly with Joseph and His mother to Nazareth, "and was subject unto them." It is written that His parents "understood not the saying which He spake unto them,"—as how should they have understood it and have lived beneath so great a weight of glory? But it is also written that "His mother kept all these sayings in her heart." And thus, in these simple words, pregnant with deepest meaning, does the narrative come to a close: "And Jesus increased in wisdom and stature, and in favour with God and man."

"Jesus increased!" What marvels are not involved in this saying! The whole conception of our Blessed Master's gradual realization of His own Divinity—in strictest accord though it be with the analogy of the faith once delivered to the saints—is a mystery of the faith to be approached, so to speak, on bended knees, and to be spoken of with bated breath. We can well believe that there were deep yearning thoughts in the soul of the Holy Child before His going up to Jerusalem; unopened buds, so to speak, of undefined hope and wondering apprehension. And yet, as it might seem, these thoughts came not to a head, and these buds did not blossom, until Jesus—now deeply thoughtful and early versed in the Scriptures—found Himself in His Father's house in Jerusalem. Then, as it would appear, in the asking and answering of questions light descended, if not the full blaze of light which should shine afterwards, yet such light as scarcely had dawned before, light as to His mission upon earth, light as to the transcendent truth that He, even He, was the Christ, the Son of the Living God,—the result being that He spoke to Joseph and to His mother the amazing words: "Wist ye not that I must be about My Father's business?" The Christian, lost else in a very maze of wonder, takes his stand on those words, "Jesus increased." He "increased in wisdom." It is then probable also that He increased in knowledge of Himself. But, so far as we can judge, the Holy Child's first great stride in self-knowledge might seem to have been made, once for all, when He spoke the words, "Wist ye not that I must be about My Father's business?"

And now suffer me to ask, this history which we have sought briefly to study together, with the great thoughts arising out of it, has it or has it not a practical meaning for us? Such a meaning, my dear brethren, it ought to have. Yes; we all, even in the period of early youth, ought to attain, in humble imitation of our Lord and Master, to some degree of self-knowledge. We also, at an early age, ought in our turn to realize that God is our Father, and that nothing becomes us so well as to love to be in His house and about His business. Ask yourselves earnestly, then, has that great thought to which the Boy Saviour gave expression in the Temple gained as yet any real entrance into your hearts? It is a blessed thing to have a fixed purpose in life; a most blessed thing to serve God with the service of a son. Oh pray for such a purpose here and now, if it be only with a momentary uplifting of your heart to God!

And further I would say, let us not go to our homes this day without fresh grounds for love and adoration. Memories have been stirred for us of a light boyish figure standing in the Temple, which ought to draw forth afresh, as it were, our glad obedience and our adoring homage. Seek by the Holy Spirit's aid to be about your Father's business; and yet, like your most Blessed Redeemer, do not fail to fulfil all sweet home duties, all your allotted earthly tasks. So, whilst you do the work which is given you to do, shall you be about your Father's business now and ever.

IV.
THE COMING UNTO A PERFECT MAN.

THE COMING UNTO A PERFECT MAN.

St. Luke ii. 52.

"*And Jesus increased in wisdom, and stature, and in favour with God and man.*"

IN God there can be neither increase nor decrease. So then the words "Jesus increased" are in themselves sufficient to prove to us that the Lord Jesus is here spoken of as man and not as God. And when once we have grasped firmly the truth of the manhood of the Lord of all, then the fact of His bodily growth, and even of His mental growth, need not surprise us, is on the contrary to be taken for granted, so that we can hear unmoved (except by admiration at so great humility) the words, "Jesus increased in wisdom and stature." Yes, if only we discern that the manhood and Godhead were united in the Lord Jesus, and yet each had an essential existence, we may apprehend without much difficulty (though not without ever increasing wonder and admiration) that the growth of the Lord's human mind kept pace with the growth of His human body. And again, that the Lord Jesus should have "increased in favour with man," may seem only reasonable and in accordance with experience, for parents often see their children (faulty as these may be) valued by friends more highly as they leave childhood farther behind them. But that which perhaps may appear harder at first to understand is the fact that the Lord Jesus, He who was ever without fault, should have actually "increased in favour with God," because this implies moral and spiritual growth, or growth of the human soul or of the moral principle. Yet truly the difficulty (I do not say the wonder and the boundless condescension, but the difficulty) even here is one of our own creating. For as the Lord of all had a human body and a human mind, so also did He possess a human soul, concerning which it is written, "Thou shalt make His soul an offering for sin:" and why, it may well be asked, on what ground, should the Lord's human soul have been alone debarred from progress?

And if it be objected that our Lord was perfect already in soul as a child, and that consequently in His case there was no room for any spiritual advance or progress, the simple answer will run thus : " True, He was perfect in soul at the first according to the perfection of childhood, but *only* perfect with the perfection of the child." Now if the child nature, the child soul, be the highest, why are any suffered to go beyond it? But in truth, and beyond all doubt, brethren, highly pleasing to God as are the innocence and simple faith of children, yet may not the holiest of these be compared in the sight of God with one who has "come unto a perfect man, unto the measure of the stature of the fulness of Christ ;" and so might not even the Child Christ Himself call forth God's favour in so full and perfect a degree as the same Christ when come to the fulness of His mental and moral stature. Who does not know that before a child in God can become a " perfect man," a great and silent growth must take place in many respects within the soul? Verily in our Lord's Godhead there could be no growth, and no increase. But in His manhood, He, like all thoughtful amiable and godly children who are gifted with health, would increase naturally in stature, in wisdom, in favour with man, and in favour with God,—only that His case is of course essentially different from theirs, inasmuch as they are all partakers of a fallen nature, and He was as Adam before the fall, only susceptible of that increase which comes with natural growth and ripening.

The text gives us a rare insight into the home life of Jesus of Nazareth. It tells us, as we may all easily discern, of four distinct kinds of growth in the Saviour.

First, then, very briefly, let me speak of the actual growth in stature. That is a simple matter truly, and a plain, suggestive only of Immanuel the Virgin's Son, nourished up like other children, as it is written, "Butter and honey shall He eat," and gradually maturing much as our own children spring up around us. Birthdays would come round for Him as for other children,—little feasts, it is likely, of glad affection. The childish speeches of the Holy Child Jesus would be treasured up, we cannot doubt, nay, we even know, by His mother Mary, even as our children's sayings are delighted in now by their mothers: in the Virgin's case there is a special record that she "kept all these sayings in her heart" (S. Luke ii. 51). And we may well suppose that the Child Saviour's words and speeches would surpass all that is most delightful in Christian childhood, as it may be known to us. And then would come boyhood, a boyhood fraught with modesty, thoughtfulness, affectionate obedience, and all winning ways. And if it pleases us so to do, we may lawfully picture the Boy Saviour to our minds as helpful to His foster-father Joseph in his occupation of a carpenter, and in all ways seeking to promote the good of his nearest and dearest upon earth. Then would come in a natural succession, the Lord's fresh youth and early manhood, and finally the ripe full prime of life; His human brain all the while gathering strength, His human heart intensifying trust, reverence, and affection. And all these several periods of growth found our glorious Master still utterly obscure and unknown to the world, in Nazareth. We may well marvel at His sacred patience, at His marvellous long-suffering. Souls to all seeming were perishing; God's work, it might be said, remained undone; but the Saviour awaited patiently His Heavenly Father's signal to appear unto men. This long waiting doubtless formed part of our Great Master's trial. Surely the fiery glow and ardour of youth, the desire to be up and doing, were not unknown to Jesus of Nazareth; and to Him not least will apply the words of the Psalmist, "I waited patiently for the Lord."

And how shall we best realize, beloved, the growth of the Lord Jesus in wisdom? Here let me descend to what may seem to some of you minute particulars, familiar instances. Verily, then, Jesus, like unto other children, had, it is probable, to be taught His very letters. Doubtless He had also to be shown how to use aright His foster-father's tools of carpentering. Of a surety the Saviour of mankind, like all His fellow-men, passed through "the day of small things." Thus we behold Him at the age of twelve questioning with the doctors, asking questions of those men whose successors He knew so well how to instruct. Indeed, we may say that the Lord Jesus up to the age of thirty was a learner rather than a teacher. He was a worshipper in the country synagogue. His human mind was gathering instruction all the while. And what though there was no school of the prophets at hand, no special earthly advantages for the acquirement of learning, would not the very flowers of the field, and the stars in the sky, and Joseph and Mary, the appointed earthly guardians of the Saviour's youth, minister to the instruction of Him to whom "God gave not the Spirit by measure"? We may picture to ourselves the Child Christ praying frequently to His Heavenly Father and studying the writings of His own inspired servants the prophets. He increased in wisdom, both in heavenly wisdom and in the wisdom of this world. And by this last I mean that the Lord Jesus, like unto other men, to sinful men, would increase in all useful knowledge, in practical wisdom, and in experience. In a word, at the first He would be a child in earthly wisdom, then the boy, and then the youth, and finally the man. At the first also, we may dare to say it, He would be a child in heavenly wisdom and only afterwards a perfect man.

Now let us endeavour to understand those words, "Jesus increased in favour with man." Herein doubtless is a signal proof of our Lord's great human amiability and sweetness of heart. We may justly think of Him in Nazareth as a dutiful and a most loving Son, as an affectionate companion to His friends, as bright and genial with all men, as respectful and reverential even to His elders. It would seem in fine that Jesus won the love of His fellow-men until He ran counter to their prejudices. And surely this happy blessed fact is recorded in order to teach us what religion ought to make us; namely, winning, amiable, affectionate, free from bitterness, free from all that is forbidding or morose. And inasmuch as "Jesus increased in favour with man," we are, I should say, plainly to understand that our Master became more and more obliging, more and more serviceable and delightful to others, more considerate, more altogether pleasing and winning, as He advanced in years. Could any thing have shown the social, friendly, loving spirit of the Lord Jesus more strikingly than the fact that His first public appearance and manifestation of power took place at a marriage-feast?

And once more, brethren, "Jesus increased in favour with God." That is really to say that there was moral and spiritual growth in His human soul. Now if it be asked, what is the *moral* growth of the soul? it may be answered simply, an ever widening and deepening love and practice of integrity, righteousness, moral courage, and the like qualities, and at the same time an ever-deepening and widening detestation of all things base and tending to a lie. These things have to do with the moral growth of the soul, of the human soul of the Lord Jesus, as indeed of any other soul. And further, if it be asked, what is meant by the *spiritual* growth of the soul? it may be answered as simply, a steady gradual deepening in holiness, in sweetness of disposition, in love, meekness, self-denial, faith, apprehension of things divine, purity, and grace.

And in all these respects, moral and spiritual equally, there was doubtless a quiet growth in our Lord's human soul whilst He abode on earth. It may not be easy to trace the growth of the human soul of the Lord of all, but of the broad fact that grow it did we have assurance in the great words, "Jesus increased in favour with God." And if we look thoughtfully and reverently into the Word of God, the fact will, I think, become more and more apparent to us. Thus, for instance, as a child our Lord would seem to have shown mainly or perspicuously the childlike virtues of reverence for old age as witnessed in His behaviour to the doctors in the Temple, and of obedience towards parents, as it is recorded of Him that He was subject to Joseph and Mary. But when come to man's estate our Blessed Master showed forth a thousand glorious qualities besides, such as sacred patience—hardly to be looked for in a child—the most large-hearted and unbounded generosity, unflinching moral courage—scarcely to be reckoned among childlike virtues—untiring fortitude and matchless equanimity, and boundless self-devotion. Thus the reverence of childhood for old age deepened into reverence for all high and holy things. And the obedience of childhood to earthly parents deepened into perfect obedience to His Heavenly Father's will, even "the obedience unto death."

Thus have I spoken very briefly, and I trust not irreverently, on a subject full of beauty and of infinite wonder,—the growth of the Lord Jesus in Nazareth in body, mind, and soul. When a few thoughts have thus been hazarded, then it is that we best see how little can be known at this present time concerning the home life of the Lord of all in Nazareth; how much, how very much, remains to be learnt by us hereafter in the world to come. This which I have set before you is, as it were, but the plucking of one or two ears of wheat in a field full of standing corn as yet unreaped by man. It remains now, with the Holy Spirit's aid, to apply what has been said for our own spiritual benefit and instruction.

So then let me ask whether we dare to hope that there is in us any increase or growth corresponding in some faint degree with the increase—the several forms of increase—in the manhood of the Lord Jesus? First, I ask, may we hope that as the years go by, there is in us any increase of wisdom? Doubtless, brethren, God would have us to use our minds, use them in the attainment of earthly and of heavenly wisdom. I do not mean of course that we are all to be great scholars or practised theologians, but simply that we are to profit generally by experience, to correct our faults, to learn a little more of God's world, and above all, to learn to know God Himself ever more truly. It is a disgrace to us if in respect of these plain things we do not grow in wisdom, since only carelessness can hinder our advance. "The fear of the Lord is the beginning of wisdom." And to increase in wisdom in this highest sense is to learn to love God more and more. Let none of us indeed despise honest, useful, or delightful earthly wisdom. But above all, let us seek to increase in the only wisdom which is essential to the soul; namely, the knowledge which is of the heart, and not merely or mainly of the head. And with this object, let us read our Bibles, and let us pray fervently and frequently, nay constantly. "If any of you lack wisdom, let him ask of God, . . . and it shall be given him."

And next let me ask, brethren, may we hope that we have increased in favour with man? And here let us be honest with ourselves. Christ our Master was lovable, as we have discerned, in the highest degree. What then are we? Does our religion induce us to be amiable, to be unselfish, to be obliging? And if we have lost men's favour, or if unhappily we have never gained it, then should we ask ourselves most seriously why that is so. Then let us apprehend with reason that the fault is likely to be in ourselves, in our want of obligingness, of friendliness, of amiability; and let us reflect with sorrow how unlike we are to the Lord Jesus, who "increased in favour with man."

And to pass on : Dare we hope that we have increased in favour with God? May we hope that there has been, that there is now going on in us, any moral and spiritual growth whatever? Are we getting gradually the mastery over our passions and temptations? Do we "abhor that which is evil and cleave to that which is good"? In other words, do we increasingly love the right and hate the wrong? Do we earnestly, yea, passionately even, desire to follow in the footsteps of our Blessed Master, of Jesus the Son of Man, to "come (at length) unto a perfect man, unto the measure of the stature of the fulness of Christ"? Are we more hearty in prayer than we used to be? Do we come more frequently and more humbly to partake spiritually of the Lord's sacred flesh and blood? Are we purer, braver, more lowly and patient, more trusting and less worldly than in time past? Do we see in ourselves any improvement in temper, habits, and self-control?

Here be many questions, beloved. Are we dismayed by them? That may well be so. And yet it is certain that growth is the needful condition of the accepted soul before God. "The manifestation of the

Spirit is given to every man to profit withal." And this is certainly God's will, that as Christ the Lord of all manifested as man a constant, gradual growth in all good, so we should "grow up into Him in all things."

V.
GROWTH IN QUIETNESS.

GROWTH IN QUIETNESS.

Isaiah liii. part of ver. 2.

"*He shall grow up before Him as a tender plant, and as a root out of a dry ground.*"

THE words of the text set forth our Lord's growth, His human growth of mind and body and soul, after a fashion of their own, by a very interesting comparison. In the text the Son of Man is described as a tender plant growing up before God, and as a root out of a dry ground. Now, such as is the manner of growth of a plant, even such also was the manner of growth of the Lord Jesus: "first the blade, then the ear, after that the full corn in the ear." It was a quiet, continuous growth. And if one plant, my brethren, were to be chosen above another as a type of "the Holy One and the Just," then, perhaps, might the lily for its spotlessness, or the rose for its many perfections, be the one so honoured: as it is written (Canticles ii. 1), "I am the rose of Sharon, and the lily of the valleys :" as it is written again (Hosea xiv. 5), " He shall grow as the lily ;" or else might the fruitful and spreading vine be aptly chosen, because that is the plant with which our Lord most frequently compared Himself. Rose, lily, vine, or ear of wheat, it matters not on which of these we fix our choice, so that we see in their silent, gradual growth a type of the growth of our Master Christ.

But are rose and lily too bright and lovely, perhaps, to serve as types of that "tender plant"? Might not the weeping willow or the sombre yew-tree seem fitter types of Him who is called "a man of sorrows and acquainted with grief"? Nay, brethren, our dear Master was not always thus sorrowful. Neither need we be daunted and restricted in our choice of fairest plants wherewith to compare our Saviour, by the chastened description of Him which follows close upon the text. The prophet proceeds indeed to say, "He hath no form nor comeliness ; and when we shall see Him, there is no beauty that we should desire Him." But hereby doubtless is only meant that our Lord's appearance should not answer to Oriental notions of majestic beauty; that is, would present no splendour, pomp, might, glory, wherewith to dazzle beholders. It is in no way denied that our Lord's countenance should be noble, being glorified, as it were, by the soul within. And accordingly all Christian painters of our Lord's sacred person have striven to place on the canvas their ideal; that is, their most deeply-felt sense of spiritual or of highest beauty. If it be further asked, what is the meaning, then, of those other mournful words, " His visage was so marred more than any man, and His form more than the sons of men "? It may be well answered that these sad words apply in all likelihood to Him on whose face the soldiers did spit, to the scourged, the buffeted, the crowned with thorns, the crucified, to Him who was pierced with a spear, but *not* to the Lord Jesus who dwelt in peaceful Nazareth, and grew up like a tender plant before His Heavenly Father. It is with the same Lord, indeed, "Christ crucified," but at a period long prior to His crucifixion, that we are now dealing. So let us go back to Him in His tender youth.

The growth, then, of the Lord Jesus in peaceful Nazareth was of a quiet and, as it were, a silent order, as it is written: "He shall not cry, nor lift up, nor cause His voice to be heard in the street." As a tender plant did the Lord Jesus grow in sweet and sober quietness before His gracious Heavenly Father—stem, leaves, and blossoms, slowly unfolding more and ever

F

more of loveliness and sweetness. His was no hasty sudden growth like that of the gourd in one night, but a gradual, a reasonable, a healthful growth of body, mind, and soul ; a growth extending over many years, like that of some rare plant which should bloom but once in a man's lifetime. The Lord Jesus may be compared to a plant that is at once tender and hardy, delicate and fragrant as the rose or lily of the valley, fruitful as the vine or ear of wheat, strong and mighty as the cedars of Lebanon.

And by the last words of the text, "As a root out of a dry ground," may be understood doubtless the spiritual dryness of the soil whence the Lord Jesus sprang. For, was not our Blessed Master born in Judea? And did He not dwell in Galilee, in that small mountain land, though it was God's own chosen province, where Pharisees and Sadducees had overlaid or trampled out well nigh each spark of spiritual hope and promise? And were not the inhabitants of Nazareth, where He was "brought up," held in great contempt, so that "an Israelite indeed in whom there was no guile," even Nathanael, could ask, "Can any good thing come out of Nazareth?" And did not our Blessed Lord's fellow-townsmen or fellow-villagers give proof of their dryness and hardness of heart by twice rejecting Him when in later life He twice came graciously preaching the Word of Promise in their ear? So, then, brethren, out of a dry and truly unspiritual soil, this root of David, this lily, this rose of Sharon, this vine, even our blessed Redeemer, sprang and grew gradually to full human perfection. It may be also that one other reason why our Lord is here compared to a root out of a dry ground may arise from the circumstance that He, "the root of David," had sprung from a line which though royal was shorn of all its earthly glory. David's royal line had become nearly extinct, or, at the least, in a manner dry. David's descendants were now few and no longer numbered among the great, when "as a root out of a dry ground" this mightiest Son of David, after thirty years of slow ripening, burst into glorious bloom, into richest fruit, and manifested Himself to men as the Messiah by His first miracle of changing water into wine and by all the countless wonders that ensued.

So, then, the ground was dry, but heavenly dews watered the plant, and heaven's own sunshine quickened it. The ground was dry, but the Virgin mother of our Lord and His foster-father, just Joseph, did doubtless all that in them lay to shelter and comfort this tender plant. The ground was dry, but an atmosphere of love and holiness surrounded this sweetest of plants upon the face of the whole earth. The ground was dry, but the grace of God was upon the plant, as it is written: "God giveth not the Spirit by measure unto Him." And as each living bud opened out, as each tender leaf unfolded, there was surely joy in one household in Nazareth. even that of Joseph and Mary, and surely joy among the angels of God also. And what though fury and curses and a dreadful death awaited our gracious Redeemer at the hands of His fellow-countrymen, yet there, in the sacred shelter of home, peace and human affection were His at least. The Son of Man has indeed said, "A prophet is not without honour, but in his own country, and among his own kin, and in his own house." But our hearts may well assure us that not to Mary and Joseph would this reproach extend, though it applied but too truly to our Lord's near kinsmen at a later day, concerning whom it is written, "for neither did His brethren believe in Him." But to love our Blessed Lord, and even to honour Him as Jesus, the Son of Joseph, was one thing; to acknowledge Him as Messiah the Prince, was quite another, and ran counter to all the dearest convictions and prepossessions of the Jewish heart. Loved as man at least He was, and loved we should desire to be.

Now, then, dear brethren, let me go on to point out that the great mark of a Christian life, like that of the tender plant in Nazareth, is growth, and moreover, growth in quietness. We may have dreamt mayhap that it was otherwise. If so, let us awake fully to the truth. Some of us may have conceived that a rapid, sudden spiritual uprising is looked for inevitably and invariably at our hands by God our Saviour. But that is not so. Love, trust, faith, obedience; and again, in another walk of life, honesty, truthfulness, kindness, purity,—these things, brethren, spring not to light in the heart at one burst, but should gradually germinate and grow within us. When did men ever see, save it may be in some juggler's trick, a rose-tree put forth roses whilst they gazed upon it? True spiritual growth resembles the growth of the plant, and so is it naturally and necessarily gradual. They who demand as a proof of the soul's life before God the appearance in one and the same moment of the stem, leaves, blossom, and fruit of the plant of grace, are as unreasonable as very children, who in their haste to make a show should plant in their little gardens gay flowers severed from the root, which for awhile might have a bright appearance, but would soon fade and fall away. Time and a root are needed for all true, all genuine, all enduring growth.

There are various stages in the growth of a natural plant, none of which can be missed without great loss. There are stem, bud, and leaf, each in turn requiring a special perfection of its own, so many inferior and secondary perfections, as it were, before the sweet blossom or crowning glory of the fruit be attained to. Thus, also, in Christians who would follow in their Master's footsteps, there ought to be some faint and distant measure of the perfection of childhood, and again, of that of youth, before the crowning measure of fulness of Christian manhood or womanhood be attained to. For the babe is not the man in Christ Jesus. It is true, God be praised, that where the knowledge and the love of God have been long absent, but where repentance and faith are notwithstanding deep in later life, there those earlier stages of soul-ripening may be dispensed with, so far as salvation is concerned, but never without detriment—never without loss and injury, both to God's glory and the soul, and consequent grief of heart to the penitent sinner.

The system under which we live before God, dear brethren, as members of the Church of England, is not a forcing system. God forbid! Our spiritual mother does not encourage us to stake our all upon a sudden hothouse outburst of excitement. Yet is she

—God be praised for it!—no "dry ground." Having placed us as infants in the Lord's fenced vineyard, in the kingdom of God, by Christian baptism, she claims from Christian parents that they should train and prune, nourish and comfort, their little ones so as to bring them into closest likeness, as far as may be, to that "tender plant" which grew up before God of old in Nazareth: remembering Who it is that dwells in all regenerate children—even God, the Holy Ghost, and, therefore dealing hopefully and trustfully with them, looking for a gradual and constant growth in grace on their part, rather than for the attainment of perfection at a single bound. Never indeed—we know it very well—can we attain here on earth to perfection, or any thing that even distantly resembles it in our own sight. But aim after it we may and should. For what said our Blessed Lord? "Be ye therefore perfect, even as your Father which is in Heaven is perfect." This is our rule; this is the standard set before us, though doubtless it should evermore convince us that we are miserable sinners, looking only for acceptance in the Beloved.

Well, then, dear brethren,—now, give me your redoubled attention,—this is the sum of the matter: are we, or are we not, at this present time growing up before God as a tender plant? Our Lord's growth may be said, perhaps, to have come to an end in a mere human sense in the attainment of absolute perfection when He was about thirty years of age, though even this may seem questionable in the light of the saying, " It became Him (even the Father) to make the Captain of men's salvation perfect through sufferings" (Heb. ii. 10). But our growth—that is, the growth of our soul—can never end at any period of our earthly life. For even the aged may grow daily and hourly in grace, and their last blossoms may be more gracious than their early bloom; their last fruits may be sweeter and riper than the fruits of their early years. God grant it be so for some of us here present! But, alas! there is a growth in evil as well as a growth in godliness. How is it with us? Are we growing up and on as tender plants, or are we, alas! even as tares before God? Do our hearts grow harder, for this may be so, and our dispositions more worldly, more selfish, or envious, or greedy of gain, or exacting, as we advance in years? God forbid that it should be so! But we must search well our own hearts. Or, does Christ dwell more and more in our hearts by faith? Again, I ask, beloved brethren, how is it with us morally and spiritually? For instance, are we more truthful and honest than in the past? Are we more anxious to obey Christ our Master's commands? Are we more unselfish and contented? Are we more prayerful? Are we more faithful, loving, and lowly? Are we, in a word, more heavenly-minded? And, in particular, are we conquerors in increasing measure of those evil tempers which more or less continually assail us? For even by this small test may we in some measure learn to know whether our souls have grown and are growing in grace.

Oh, bitter thought, perhaps, for some of us now come to full age, that whereas we should be nearer and dearer to God than when we were children (even as our Master Christ, as man, " increased in favour with God,") we are become too possibly comparative strangers and aliens to the covenant of God. Oh, sad, deeply sad, if when God demands from us blossom and fruit, heartfelt devotion and all-embracing charity, our sap, the life of the soul, be found to have dried up within us! Yea, most sad, if the soul have not grown with the growth of mind and body, but has rather gradually become dwarfed and stunted! Oh mockery to speak of any crowning glory in connexion with the declining years of too many careless Christians! What says the Word of God to such? " Be troubled, ye careless ones." " Make you a new heart and a new spirit: for why will ye die, O house of Israel?" Great is your call. It is not only Christ growing up before the Father as a tender plant in Nazareth who calls you lovingly unto Himself, but it is " Christ crucified," it is Christ who died upon the tree to save you from your sins, it is Christ who was " wounded for our transgressions" and " bruised for our iniquities," it is Christ on whom the Lord hath laid the iniquity of us all, it is Christ our Saviour who in the salvation of sinners " shall see of the travail of His soul and be satisfied," Christ the Lamb of God whose soul is made an offering for sin. But if you dare humbly to trust that you are the faulty but loving servants of Christ, then, brethren, let growth in quietness be your aim and your mark, not a noisy, flaunting religion, loud and boastful, but rather, still earnest, continuous, and advancing, even such a moral and spiritual growth of the soul as our Blessed Saviour underwent before us. So shall you be more and more conformed to His image. So shall your modest blossoms, your poor fruits, become brighter and richer and fuller, and yet leave you trusting only in your Redeemer's merits and in His living mediation on your behalf.

VI.
OUR LORD BELOVED OF MEN.

OUR LORD BELOVED OF MEN.

St. Luke ii. part of ver. 52.
"*Jesus increased . . . in favour with . . . man.*"

HERE we have a fact revealed to us concerning our Blessed Redeemer which is not a little interesting and consoling. For is it not in truth consoling to learn, on the authority of God's Word, that He who in later life was "despised and rejected of men," should, like Samuel before Him, have increased in favour with man from boyhood onward? It would seem that men loved our Saviour well until He ran counter to their prejudices! As yet the world hated Him not, for the excellent reason that hitherto He had not testified of it that "the works thereof are evil." It is written indeed in S. John's Gospel, "He came unto His own, and His own received Him not;" but this statement can apply in strictness only to the time of our Lord's public ministry when He disappointed worldly men in their expectations of a conquering Messiah. Up to the age of thirty Jesus would seem to have been loved increasingly, not indeed by the generality of His countrymen, who knew Him not, but by His friends and acquaintance, even by the inhabitants of Nazareth where He was "brought up."

And in the revealed fact that Jesus increased in favour with those around Him, we may, I think, discern true cause for rejoicing. For if the Saviour's life was not altogether joyless, then does a weight seem lifted from off our spirits. Then may a fitting place be found on earth for innocent joy and laughter, for the innocent delights of Christian art and science. Doubtless the sad impending end may have cast a certain shadow before it over our dear Master's early days, yet was His life, so much seems clear, not wholly one of gloom and sadness. Those deeply touching words of Isaiah, "A man of sorrows and acquainted with grief," may hardly seem to have met with their fulfilment in peaceful Nazareth. For over and above the joyous influence exercised by the many natural glories of Palestine, the deep blue sky, the sunshine, the flowers in a rich abundance, the mountains, the distant view of the Mediterranean Sea as beheld from the heights above Nazareth—all so many manifestations to our beloved Master of His Father's bounteous care —over and above all these things, I say, the Saviour's life on earth was surely cheered by the sunshine of human affection. Not merely because Jesus dwelt in a favoured spot of that fair world which He had made, but rather because all who drew near to Him loved Him, would the Lord of all enjoy His lowly share of earthly gladness. The Saviour spending thirty uneventful years in the mountain city of Nazareth as the carpenter's Son with His mother Mary, need not excite our pity—rather our adoring wonder—that He, the Father's Son, should have deigned to live the ordinary life of man with man, so setting to all ages an example of calm contentment in a lowly lot. All His surroundings, doubtless, would be very humble. Not only was the Lord of all reputed to be a carpenter's Son, but further He would seem actually to have followed His foster-father's trade, so ennobling labour, as appears from these words in S. Mark's Gospel (6th chapter and 3rd verse):—"Is not this the carpenter, the Son of Mary?" And, moreover, the Lord's companions in Nazareth would be mostly poor men, dependent for a livelihood on their scanty fig-trees and strips of corn-land, and vineyard, and olive-garden, mere patches on the mountain side. But whether the dwellers in Nazareth were poor or well to do in this world's goods, it is pleasant, my brethren, it is consoling to think of the good will felt by them towards our Lord during many, many years.

That good will the Lord Jesus would seem to have ever conciliated where possible. Thus—to turn for an instant to the single incident revealed to us in our Lord's boyhood—it would appear that the behaviour of the Holy Child Jesus at the age of twelve towards the doctors in the Temple was such as to win their personal favour and regard. Not His to assume any superiority over those venerable Jewish teachers. Not His to teach them save in the modest form of question and reply. And in connexion with that early visit to Jerusalem, let me bring to your notice what seems a strong incidental proof of our Lord's social disposition in youth. It is written, "But they (His parents) supposing Him to have been in the company, went a day's journey; and they sought Him among their kinsfolk and acquaintance." Why sought they Him among their kinsfolk and acquaintance? The inference is obvious. Because the Holy Child was wont to frequent their society.

So then, sociability or friendliness, as well as modesty and thoughtfulness, marked our Saviour as a boy, and doubtless these qualities never left Him. And the strongest, the most conclusive testimony is borne to our Lord's amiability in that brief and simple statement of the text, "Jesus increased in favour with man." More so, perhaps, than may at first sight appear to all of us; for we may too lightly assume, without much reflection, that as a matter of course man's favour attends on those who are eminently holy. But that is not so. A one-sided devotion never yet sufficed to win men's favour. The truth is that men are disposed ordinarily to be daunted by exalted saintliness. Our Master's saintliness, however, was not counted to Him as a crime by men, did not stand as a barrier between Him and men's affection, as it so easily might have done, and that because He was doubtless perfectly amiable as well as perfectly holy, because He loved both God and man.

It is a matter of sad experience that saints, so far from being invariably beloved even by the well-disposed among men, are very liable to be regarded with some degree of coldness and suspicion. And for this they may perhaps sometimes justly blame their own want of human sympathy. Their rules of conduct being higher than those of other men, give to them a striking superiority, which, unless it be accompanied by real warmth and kindness of heart and manner, is too apt to be felt as galling. The careful walk of God's saints is a silent reproach to the careless, and that is well. Only, frankness and warmth of heart are qualities that seem especially called for in men and women who lead saintly lives; and not every saint of God upon earth, alas! is amiable or genial, or disposed to give others full credit for good intentions where that is possible. And, therefore, not every saintly man or woman is beloved, or, what is more, goes the way to be beloved. Not every saint or faithful Christian is like our Lord in respect of increasing in favour with man as well as God.

Some good men, alas! are well contented, not so much as to aim even at being in favour with their brethren upon earth, on the strength of such passages as the following: "Woe unto you, when all men shall speak well of you!" And again, "Ye shall be hated of all men for My name's sake." And once more: "Blessed are ye when men shall revile you, and persecute you, and shall say all manner of evil against you falsely for My sake." But surely these three passages—to take them one by one—do but instruct us when rightly understood, first, that the applause of men may lightly prove a snare; for what else but this is the true signification of the words, " Woe unto you when all men shall speak well of you"? or secondly, that, as a matter of fact, Jews and heathen men would hate professing Christians; and why attribute any further meaning than this to the words, "Ye shall be hated of all men for My name's sake"? or lastly, that if unhappily the favour of men should forsake us in the performance of our bounden duty, God will more than make good our loss to us; and what else but this is the force of those fuller words, " Blessed are ye when men shall revile you, and persecute you, and shall say all manner of evil against you falsely for My sake?" Truly there is nothing, absolutely nothing, in all this to make us indifferent to the good will and even the favour of our brother Christians. And since the Lord of all aimed at securing men's favour, and actually did secure it, His saints, it seems to me, should plainly aim at nothing less. As we increase in favour with God, so should we honestly strive, brethren, duty permitting, to increase in favour with man also. Of course the loss of men's good will may be forced upon us by duty, and so by way of consolation it is written, " Rejoice ye in that day and leap for joy; for behold, your reward is great in heaven." But this is only said to bless and comfort him who has done all he can to avert hatred, who in vain has striven to overcome evil with good, and yet after all is hated for the Son of Man's sake.

And the way being thus cleared, suffer me to suggest broadly and without going into details, what were the probable means taken by our Lord to acquire the favour of men. The fact, the blessed fact, is alone recorded of His being increasingly beloved. We have to account for that fact as best we may. Truly then, my brethren, I think we shall not be far wrong if we seek to account for it, at least in part, by the mention of two things only; first, by the mention of a thing that our Lord must have carefully refrained from doing, and then by the mention of another thing that He doubtless most carefully observed to do. What then, our Blessed Lord, as I conceive, avoided (to judge as we fairly may of the unknown period of His life by the known), was to fix His attention perpetually, or frequently at least, on people's private faults and shortcomings. And what He observed to do (judging in like manner of the unrevealed by the revealed) was to draw out all the good that was in them, and take pleasure in that.

He who came to save that which was lost must have seen as none else could see the faults of His brother-men; and seeing these He might as man have lost patience. All mortal weakness lay unbared before His gaze. But He who saw the most made the largest allowances, saying in the garden, when His apostles slept, "The spirit truly is willing, but the flesh is weak." And this was well. For if the Son of Man had suffered His human mind to dwell solely or chiefly on the countless imperfections of men, He might soon have lost all heart to aid His fellows, or almost to associate with them. He would then, as man, have placed Himself out of sympathy with His brother-men. How easily, for instance, might the Lord have despised Peter for his over-confident spirit, or Thomas for his doubtfulness. But no; He even bore with Judas to the end.

But further, if the Lord perceived what was evil in man, He also perceived all good impulses, all generous instincts, all aspirations after that which was noble and true, all capacities for renewal in the human heart. And we may be sure that He loved to look on the good side of man. Doubtless, my dear brethren, if we may judge of our Lord's conduct during the first thirty years of His life by what we know of that conduct during the closing years,—doubtless I say He set Himself habitually to draw out and intensify all that was generous and good in men's hearts. And here, if we will, we may bear in mind, as an instance in point of what is now advanced, the Scripture narrative of Christ's interview with the woman of Samaria at Jacob's well. And once for all I may well affirm that whereas it is Satan's part to ripen buds and blossoms of sin into evil fruit, so it is the Lord's part to bring the good seed to perfection. Did our Blessed Master, for instance, ever see in any of His companions in Nazareth the faint wish to do right, we may be tolerably sure that He would seek to strengthen that faint wish and quicken it into an earnest resolve. "A bruised reed should He not break, nor quench the smoking flax," but rather "bind up that which was broken, and strengthen that which was sick." None would leave His sacred presence without having had the good that was in them cherished and upheld in some sense, consciously or unconsciously, with little of effort probably, but by a healing, sunlike influence.

To these and other like simple causes may we, I think, in the absence of direct revelation, attribute the fact of our Lord having increased in favour with man. And now, in brief conclusion, let me exhort you, beloved, to aim at resembling the Lord Jesus, at least in your faint measure, in this respect also. Study at once, that is, to be holy and to be amiable. We are not to shut ourselves up selfishly in ourselves, but we are to live for others, as ever and in all things towards God. Let us try to look on the good that is in others rather than on the evil, to be large-hearted, to be merciful, to be cheerful and feeling. And suffer your love to be drawn out afresh towards your Saviour even by these faint glimpses of His wisdom and goodness. Let us not have gazed in spirit on Nazareth even from afar without doing homage with heart and soul to earth's most gracious Redeemer.

One more thought. Should the Lord Jesus have loved so well His companions in Nazareth, and should He have no love to spare for us? Believe that from heaven He now looks on us with eyes of love, ready, nay anxious, to quicken our every good impulse, to purify our hearts by His Holy Spirit, to draw us altogether to Himself. He longs for our renewal. He desires nothing so much as our growth in grace, as our salvation. Oh that we might arise from sin and carelessness this day! Oh that we might cry from our very souls, "Behold, we come unto Thee; for Thou art the Lord our God"!

VII.
THE FATHER'S SANCTION OF THE SON'S HOME LIFE.

THE FATHER'S SANCTION OF THE SON'S HOME LIFE.

S. Luke iii. part of verses 22 and 23.

"*Thou art My beloved Son; in Thee I am well pleased. And Jesus Himself began to be about thirty years of age.*"

THIRTY years of retirement were past. Three years, or three years and a half, of active ministry were at hand. Let us wonder at the marvellous speed with which the Lord Jesus laid the eternal foundations of Christianity, taught His Heavenly Father's doctrine, and presented mankind with the inspiring example of His obedience unto death. But this so swift Saviour showed no undue haste. He waited long and patiently. Not before the age of thirty did the priests of Aaron enter on their high office. And that was doubtless one reason why the Lord Jesus took no decisive step till then. Moreover, the spectacle of an over youthful prophet would not have been edifying. So then thirty years came and went, and found the Messiah leading a peaceful, and we may even dare to hope a happy, yes, a happy human life in Nazareth.

Why should not our Blessed Master have known happiness at that time? True, unutterable woes to come may have cast their grave and awful shadows around His path. Never may we, or could He, it may be, wholly forget the Cross of Calvary! But would not also the glad presentiment of final triumph come to cheer? Ah surely yes! And then the question seems to be, which would outbalance the other, the fathomless grief, or the infinite joy? Say that our Blessed Master foresaw the coming rejection of Himself by His own nation; say that He foresaw the future rejection of Himself by countless hosts of nominal Christians; say that He foresaw all this, and more: then would He not also foresee the winning of millions of souls for God? But I speak tentatively and not as one with authority here, brethren. Who shall say how far, at this time, the sense and knowledge of these things may not have been miraculously withheld from the Man Christ Jesus, lest His human likeness to His fellows, His human liability to temptation, should be impaired. I speak only on the assumption that at least at certain seasons of youth, there was in our Lord's mind a deep prescience of coming joys and sorrows. Then you feel, dear brethren, that if the Lord Jesus foresaw the evil, He no less foresaw the good. And in your estimation, which would affect Him most keenly? You will never say, no you will scarcely say, that the evil can have outweighed the good; else might it seem as if God had vainly and to little purpose called this fair world and its inhabitants out of chaos! and as if the work of redemption had been itself a failure.

But it is conceivable that for wise purposes the full knowledge of all that was to come, whether of good or of evil, was withheld or kept back at this time from the youthful Messiah. If so, then may we perhaps fitly liken our Blessed Master in Nazareth to some mortal whose spirit should be set on slowly ripening and perfecting a work of blessing for his fellow-men, of which work he knows not the full or certain issue. And what then? Is such an one ordinarily unhappy? Is he not rather, despite of many possible anxieties, apt to be filled with glad anticipations? Ay, surely. And wherefore then might not the youthful Jesus, meditating nothing less than the world's salvation, have been joyous too? But you will say, the artist, the inventor, the would-be benefactor of mankind, be he what he may, does not contemplate self-sacrifice, and the Saviour did contemplate this. That is most true. Every way the Saviour's joy would be alloyed with much of sorrow. Deep, necessarily deep, must have been the shadows in the hidden period of our Lord's life on earth. Yet remember this, thoughts of self-sacrifice ever bring with them a heavenly if not an earthly gladness. The unselfish desire for others' good, amidst the prospect of personal sorrows, blesses like the very sunshine. And so, unless I greatly err, we may even dare to trust that there was more to cheer than to grieve in the home life of the Saviour in Nazareth.

But apart from these deep considerations, we may well think, brethren, that the home life of the Lord Jesus would be rendered happy by many things,—by His earthly mother's affection, by the fostering care of Joseph, by the love of His friends and brethren, most of all by His Heavenly Father's tenderness, which would bring with it the highest of all blessings, the very peace of God. Holiness is happiness in itself, that let us never doubt. Truly the utmost humility of judgment befits us here. The place whereon we stand is most holy ground. But we may reverently think our thoughts, and reverently too express them. And not the most vivid recollection of Isaiah's prophecy, "A man of sorrows and acquainted with grief," need constrain us to apply these touching words to the Saviour during His peaceful abode in Nazareth. Enough that this prophecy was amply fulfilled later in our Lord's active ministry, and more especially towards the close thereof. So then if it be possible, if it be in probable accordance with the very truth, but not otherwise, let us cling to this loving hope of a happy home life in Nazareth. They who love their Master Christ will rejoice to be able to think that He then was happy; and in His happiness they will only see cause for making others happy, and for daring, yes, and daring, to be happy themselves.

Some grounds for the hope that our Lord's earthly life was not altogether sad have been already touched on. But the weight of undefined gloom which besets so many Christian minds in respect of our Lord's entire earthly life is not to be scattered lightly, is perhaps only to be removed or diminished by entire outspokenness. So there is need to place before you reverently certain of the less known features of that sacred life, such as are little thought of generally and are rarely dwelt upon by teachers, but are none the less true and certain in themselves. And when once we have made allowance for the difference between heaven and earth, between the glory which the Son had with the Father "before the world was" and the common lot of mortality,—we shall I think find no special circumstances of gloom, other than may be connected with the foreknowledge of woes to come, in the home life of the Lord of all. Thus I may well ask, what mattered it that Nazareth was but a mountain town or village, or that the Lord's occupation was that of a carpenter only? As much of happiness is to be found in a village and in a lowly occupation as in great cities and in highest offices of dignity. And though indeed our Blessed Master was poor, poverty in His case was not associated with ignorance or disorder, or coarseness, which are its worst accompaniments, or even we may venture to trust with actual want, since from this last the Saviour would, it is well nigh certain, be shielded both by His trade and by the natural fertility of the country in which He dwelt.

So then, though we should never cease to marvel at the transcendent act of condescension whereby God became man, we are not justified in speaking of our Lord's life on earth as if it had been only one long string of miseries. Let us not fail to remember that sin is the chief misery and chief cause of misery for all that live, and that from sin our Saviour's life was absolutely free, though indeed a time was to come when on Him should be laid the burden of the sins of the whole world. And to pass on, it was not a miserable lot in itself to be the earthly support and comfort of a mother, and of such a mother! Indeed, what more noble duty than this of caring for His widowed mother could we have desired for our Blessed Saviour during His home life? Our Lord, with deepest reverence be it said, was a true mother's son, a sure stay, a consolation, a delight to her who had given Him birth. Again, it was not miserable to live amid a great abundance of fruits and flowers, as did the dwellers in Nazareth. Further, the colours of the glowing East, the hues of sky and earth and sea, were nothing less than glorious, so many outward tokens of a Heavenly Father's love; and by these was our Lord surrounded. For another thing, it was not miserable that the Lord Jesus should be sheltered in quiet Nazareth from oppression and strife, whereas all the chief places in His country were occupied by the conquering soldiers of Rome. Miserable, indeed! Who that dwelt in Nazareth would so much as dream that the lot of the youthful Jesus was a sad lot? Who of all the neighbours I ask, would think this, when first they beheld Him giving a helping hand in His foster-father's workshop, or when later (after that foster-father's death), they saw Him labouring for the support of His mother, then no longer young? What was there sad about it? Be sure, be very sure, brethren, that one mark of our Redeemer's home-life was sweet human contentment.

But at length, when "Jesus Himself began to be about thirty years of age," the period of peace and rest and of comparative earthly happiness had finally passed away. The example of contentment in a humble lot had by that time been given. The active stirring period of our Lord's earthly existence was about to commence. Into that life of untiring activity we cannot follow the Saviour now. Behold Him at the threshold. Behold Him at the point whence onward clamour was to take the place of peace, and deadly enmity was to supplant a mother's love. Again, I say, what a change was here! But for this very change the Lord had waited long and patiently; and when it presented itself there would be no flinching, no momentary hesitation on His part. He who had been a true son of His earthly mother was also the Eternal Son of the Father, and was ready.

And now that our Blessed Master had reached the

turning-point, so to speak, in His glorious career, now that He had left behind Him for ever the hidden or home-life in Nazareth, that life was to receive His Heavenly Father's open approbation. And the Father's approval was given after this fashion. When our Redeemer was baptized in Jordan, "the Holy Ghost descended in a bodily shape like a dove upon Him, and a voice came from heaven which said, Thou art My beloved Son; in Thee I am well pleased." In these words we have the Father's sanction of the Son's home-life. For here it is to be noted that the Son had not entered as yet upon His public ministry, and that *already* the Father was well pleased in Him. It follows surely that the past time of our Lord's life on earth had been well pleasing to His Heavenly Father. And who can wonder at it? It had pleased the Father well that at length one child of man, His own beloved Son, should have shown a perfect, an absolute, a consummate obedience in all the ordinary duties and trials of a peaceful life. Yes, this had pleased the Father well. No man had ever shown a perfect obedience before. And it is the very truth to say that our Heavenly Father's heart had yearned with a deep fatherly longing to see one stainless human mirror that could, as it were, reflect back perfectly the Divine image wherein man had been created. So then, inexpressibly well pleasing to our Heavenly Father had been the life of His beloved Son in Nazareth, giving warrant as it did of the obedience unto death, even the death of the cross, which in due time should follow for the satisfaction of the sins of the world.

And here suffer me to point out to you, beloved, that the Father's approval was declared thus openly not only for the Saviour's sake, but also as a tender encouragement to all who to the end of time should endeavour to imitate the home-life of Jesus; yea, to all without exception. O you young people that now hear me, would you be truly happy? Then aim at nothing less than to live in your faint measure such a life as was the home-life of Jesus. So shall your Heavenly Father's voice whisper encouragement to your hearts also. Long and seek to be pure as the Lord Jesus was pure, true as He was true, loving, unworldly, self-sacrificing, as was He. Copy His example in respect of industry, temperance, and contentment. Be dutiful sons and daughters like unto Him. Gather stores of grace betimes. Nourish in youth a noble aim, to work not your own will but the will of God. Thus may you best prepare yourselves for the perils and more searching trials of a life of action. And believe that the power to do your duty rests with you, since God for His part is ready. For this the Holy Ghost descended upon you in baptism. For this the sevenfold gifts of the Spirit are poured out upon you in Confirmation. For this you are strengthened by the wondrous bread and wine. Our Blessed Lord, as has been said, is the perfect mirror of His Heavenly Father's perfections; but we, though truly at the best broken and tarnished, we are to be mirrors too. And be not lightly disheartened, as if this might never be. Yes, it is possible, quite possible, for a good child or youth, despite of many shortcomings, to please God. It is possible for a good man, conscious as he must needs be of wanting forgiveness in countless ways, to please God. For in Christ, brethren, we and our imperfections are accepted with God. We have a gracious God and Father who can be pleased by the lowly, honest endeavours to serve Him of those whom His Son has redeemed. And *then*, in that time, and in that way, do we best please God, when, trusting in His Son's only merits, we model our behaviour on that of Christ our Master; and this not only during the more openly revealed period of His life, but also during the partially hidden period of His home-life in Nazareth. Would, in very deed, brethren, that our "life" were "hid with Christ in God"! Once more I say, be not lightly disheartened. To us, to us all, who take Christ for our example, the voice of our Heavenly Father shall surely whisper sweet encouragement. Yea, a time may come when the Father's approving voice may speak unto our secret souls, saying, "Thou also, for My own Son's sake, art a beloved son or daughter, and in thee, according to thy measure of obedience, I am pleased;" for a man is accepted for that which he hath and not for that which he hath not; and it is written, "Thou hast been faithful over a few things; I will make thee ruler over many things: enter thou into the joy of thy Lord."

End of the Home Life of Jesus of Nazareth.

The Temptations of Our Lord.

"Verily Thou art a God that hidest Thyself, O God of Israel, the Saviour."

INTRODUCTION.

THE temptations of the Lord Jesus, standing as they do on the very threshold of His active ministry, follow in a natural order upon the story of the Home Life in Nazareth : therefore are they here treated of. That which would seem most essential to apprehend in connexion with our Lord's temptations is still the mystery of the Twofold Nature, the central truth that He was perfect man as well as perfect God. For this reason those searching trials with which Satan assailed the Son of man were most real, which else would have been unreal. It was the manhood which was tempted as far as we can judge, to yield to sinful suggestions, or else at the least to obliterate itself. It was the manhood which alone could be tempted. And the Godhead stood aloof, did not come to the rescue. Very glorious in its grand simplicity is the Scripture narrative of our Great Master's trials. How those trials would specially affect Jesus of Nazareth rather than another has been in what follows a principal object of consideration, though it has been sought also to point out that the Lord's temptations are those of all men. Mighty is the theme, a fathomless sea. The several aspects of the truth here presented are but, so to speak, soundings along the shore.

I.
THE FIRST TEMPTATION, TO SEPARATION OF OUR LORD'S LOT FROM THAT OF HUMANITY.

THE FIRST TEMPTATION,
TO SEPARATION OF OUR LORD'S LOT FROM THAT OF HUMANITY.

S. Matthew iv. 3.

"And when the tempter came to Him, he said, If Thou be the Son of God, command that these stones be made bread."

THERE would be much to make the powers of darkness hesitate before coming to a final decision as to whether Jesus were the Son of God or not. The evidence on this momentous point might reasonably appear conflicting. For instance, the manner of the Lord's birth had been so lowly, that, in spite of the marvels attendant on that birth, the sagacity of evil powers, and of the chief of fallen spirits, once Lucifer, son of the morning, might fairly be at fault. We know indeed that hell's suspicions were at the first aroused, resulting in the murderous attempt of King Herod upon the young Child's life. But afterwards when the Lord spent thirty years of lowly retirement in Nazareth there was nothing to direct the suspicions of infernal powers anew towards the Son of man, unless it were His absolute sinlessness as child and youth. When, however, at our Lord's baptism the voice from heaven had proclaimed, "Thou art My beloved Son; in Thee I am well pleased;" then it is likely would all previous suspicions be brought to a head. And further the testimony of John the Baptist, "Behold the Lamb of God, which taketh away the sin of the world," cannot but have confirmed, we may suppose, in the mind of man's chief foe, the strong presumption that Jesus was indeed the promised Seed of the woman which was to bruise the serpent's head.

Hence, as we may well conjecture, from this twofold testimony, that of John the Baptist and the mightier testimony of the voice from heaven, arose Satan's resolution to assail the Lord Jesus with his most skilful and powerful temptations. In any case, the false security of hell's evil legions in the past would seem now to have been scattered once for all; and the terror of the foe would appear to have been aroused, lest his dominion over man should be wrested from him by this new Deliverer. Accordingly, when Satan beheld the Lord Jesus retire after His baptism into the desert, that He might prepare Himself in solitude for His life's task, he would seem to have considered that now or never must he bring all his wiles to bear upon the mysterious sinless One, and prove Him in some sense a sharer in the guilt and misery of mankind. S. Mark and S. Luke represent our Saviour as having been tempted of the devil more or less during the whole forty days of His abode in the wilderness. But S. Matthew instructs us that the tempter refrained himself, at least in a measure, until he beheld the Lord Jesus weakened by long fasting. Then, spying his opportunity, as it were, he drew nigh in the form as it should seem likely of an angel of light, or perhaps, in the first instance, only as a wayfaring man passing by that way. And the first recorded utterance of that subtle intelligence, of that tongue teeming with all mischief, was no other than this: "If Thou be the Son of God, command that these stones be made bread."

"If Thou be the Son of God!" As has been already suggested, the poor surroundings of the Lord's birth, and the very obscurity in which He had continued to live for so long a time, had probably served to shield Him in large measure from the suspicions of the powers of darkness. Besides, the whole conception of the Incarnation of the Son of God was too glorious to be entertained by meaner spirits, or possibly even by him the chief of fallen angels, except most unwillingly, and under the compulsion of what might seem irresistible proofs. For there is no natural affinity between light and darkness, between moral evil and a scheme of redemption involving such treasures of boundless love and generous self-denial.

Even now Satan would not yield blindly, as it seems, to the testimony of the voice from heaven. A loophole yet remained, it is probable, for doubt. And the spectacle of suffering from hunger presented by the Son of man in the wilderness might well trouble the mind of the chief of fallen angels. For there in the wilderness Satan beheld One who for certain was a very man. Was it possible, then, that He could in any sense be God also? Could that be the Son of the Father who was allowed thus to suffer and to hunger? And, in any case, brethren, whether Satan himself doubted or not, he sought to insinuate by subtle speech that the voice from heaven, heard in the hour of baptism, had been a delusion only. The words, "*If* Thou be the Son of God," not only expressed Satan's own possible belief in such a delusion, but, further, were designed expressly, as we can scarcely question, to plant the evil seeds of doubt in the Saviour's human mind. And thus the devil's "if," when drawn out, might run after this fashion, "Thou art not verily and indeed the Son of God; neither art Thou the One Beloved. A voice said so, it is true, but the voice did but deceive. How should the Son of God, or even the Beloved of the Father, be left to starve here in the wilderness?" Verily we may discern in this "if," brethren, a bold attempt to make the Lord Jesus as man distrustful of His Heavenly Father's goodness. In a word, in this daring "if," we may recognize a variation of the old treacherous question asked in Paradise, "Yea, hath God said?"

Notice next the word "command," my brethren. "If Thou be the Son of God, *command.*" Here we have what would appear to be a very leading point in the temptation. Behold Satan suggesting that if the Lord Jesus were indeed the Very Son of God, then should He command rather than obey and trust. Now I think we shall all easily see how ill it would have become the Son of man (Son of God though He were) to give commands. For the Son of God had emptied Himself willingly of the glory which He had with the Father before the worlds were made, and had become man, so as to yield an acceptable and perfect human obedience to the Father. And having become man, was He to command stones to be made bread because He was in need of food? No, assuredly. It plainly became the Son, as man, to yield a willing, a trustful, a perfectly patient obedience to the Father's will even in the very depths of want and misery. Had not Adam's sin in the garden been mainly a failure in obedience? See then the necessity, the absolute necessity, brethren, of there being no failure of obedience in the second Adam. And such a failure the devil plainly aimed at bringing about. For what Satan said in effect was no other than this, "Cease for one moment, at least, to be only man, and show Thyself the very God Thou art. Command, as Thou hast the right."

But what was the particular command which Satan suggested? It was, as we know, "Command that *these stones be made bread.*" Here, brethren, we may first of all say, was a temptation of the flesh. This temptation was addressed obviously to the very man Christ Jesus, to induce Him to satisfy His human hunger, His strong craving for food. And let us not forget the force of the temptation. For forty days and nights the Lord Jesus had fasted. He was now an hungred. What an exercise of self-denial was that which having the power to provide bread forbore to use it! For let Him only give an order that would hurt nobody, let Him turn but a few unprofitable stones into bread, let Him step aside a very very little from the path of entire submission, and His hunger, His terrible hunger, would be instantly appeased! That might seem most innocent in itself which the tempter here suggested, for had not the Father created all things by and for the Son? And so, might not the Son create a little bread for His own use? The Son of man who later was to gather the very elements miraculously into the form of loaves and fishes for others' sake, might He not turn stones into bread for Himself? No, brethren, He might not, for He was upon His trial now as the Son of man, perfecting all obedience by suffering even unto death, not immediately as the Son of God. And would we have had the Son of man to eat of forbidden fruit, even as Adam did eat and fell? But to command stones to be made bread for His own advantage would have been to do that which to man, as man, is forbidden. And it needs scarcely to be pointed out that whatever is forbidden to man, could have been no less forbidden to the Lord Jesus as man. The Son of God had come to live as man, and to die as man, and to yield man's acceptable and perfect obedience. He had come to exercise uttermost self-denial as man. He had come to learn obedience by suffering "though He were a Son."

Now doubtless, beloved brethren, it was the human side of our Lord's nature whereby Satan most dreaded defeat. There could be no contest with that which was Divine in our Lord; so might there be neither victory nor defeat. But if Jesus of Nazareth triumphed over all the wiles of Satan *as man*, that would be a defeat indeed for man's adversary, that would be a bruising of the serpent's head. Therefore Satan would desire to induce the Lord Jesus to forsake His manhood, and to cast Himself upon the resources of His Divinity, that is, on the supposition of His being the promised Messias, Immanuel, God with men. Only let there not be presented any longer a spectacle so repugnant to the Prince of the power of the air as that of a perfect human obedience! Any thing rather than that, surely. Was one man about to stand at last, and in some sense to raise the fallen race of Adam, and to restore it to God's favour by a perfect human obedience? This was Satan's most just fear. Therefore, said he, "If Thou be the Son of God, command that these stones be made bread." " Show Thyself (in other words), not as the man, but as the God." Thus was our great Master tempted to sacrifice His promised work whereby He sought to identify Himself with lost humanity.

But our blessed Lord did not yield to this subtle suggestion. "He answered and said, It is written, Man shall not live by bread alone, but by every word that proceedeth out of the mouth of God." Do you notice, brethren, "*Man* shall not live by bread alone"? Satan had made appeal to the hidden God. It was the man Christ Jesus who gave answer. It was the man who exercised self-denial. It was the man who submitted to be guided by the written word. It was the man who would endure patiently unto the end all that it should please the Father to lay upon Him in the way of suffering. And unless the Father sent bread, the Son would not command it—not even to save His life. Behold Satan baffled!

Oh what ruin for us would that have been, my brethren, we may dare to say, what extremest injury every way, if Christ the Lord had helped Himself by any word of command out of His great strait of hunger in the wilderness—if He had trusted in His own right hand rather than in His Father's goodness! For not to glance at deeper and unutterable loss, even the apparent fall of the second Adam, or at least the resignation of His mighty work of Redemption, what man of us, when seeking to resist some fierce craving of the flesh, could then have been strengthened by the Lord's example? But now we can say, when we are tempted, "We will wait patiently with our Master Christ until it shall please our Heavenly Father to supply our needs, and we will not help ourselves by forbidden methods of any kind, or display want of trust in Divine Providence."

Yea, strong in Christ, let us withstand the many temptations of the flesh with which Satan assails us. O you young people more especially, strengthen yourselves, by your Saviour's example, for your conflict with the sinful lusts of the flesh. Your trials and temptations shall only redound to the glory of God and to the good of your souls, if you endeavour to meet them honestly and sincerely as Christ your Master met them, with a firm trust in your Heavenly Father's goodness, and with a resolute obedience to His will. The Holy Spirit will protect you, if you open your hearts to His good influences. Satan need not conquer you. You may be "more than conquerors" in Christ. But it is grievous to think that some of you are only too likely to fall hereafter into some deadly sins of the flesh, even into sins of uncleanness or impurity, to name at once the very worst of these. "It is impossible but that offences will come : but woe unto him through whom they come."

Again I say to you, to all, Learn by your Saviour's example that obedience to your Heavenly Father means more than a fulfilment of light and pleasant duties means, more than the obedience of the child to its parents when desired to do that in which it takes delight, means obedience in painful duties, obedience in self-denial, obedience under severe trials, under searching temptations. Behold in Christ our great example. Did our Master Christ decline to command stones to be made bread? Then do you also decline to seize upon forbidden fruit of any kind. Did your Master Christ deny His very appetite? Then do you deny your natural appetites also. Yes; avail yourselves, brethren, of this godly Lenten season, instituted by the Church of Christ in memory of her Saviour's fast in the wilderness, to exercise some self-denial in respect of food and of ordinary pleasure. Seek to baffle Satan in respect of this first and grievous temptation. Above all, let purity appear in your eyes that which it is in God's sight, the choicest and most needful of all virtues. Willingly forego all else, if you can compass this. Seize on nothing that is withheld from you by law or duty. So then, I say, strong in the example of Christ the Lord, learn to baffle Satan when he next assails you with any temptation of the flesh. Your Lord fights in you, with you, and for you. The Holy Spirit shall protect you. Be brave, be pure, be strong, be self-denying. Look to God's Word for counsel, and trust in God. Pray for light, for guidance, for strength, in the name of Christ Jesus your Master. So shall you prevail.

II

THE SECOND TEMPTATION, TO THE VINDICATION OF OUR LORD'S MESSIAHSHIP.

THE SECOND TEMPTATION,
TO THE VINDICATION OF OUR LORD'S MESSIAHSHIP.

S. Matthew iv. 5, 6.

"*Then the devil taketh Him up into the holy city, and setteth Him on a pinnacle of the temple, and saith unto Him, If Thou be the Son of God, cast Thyself down: for it is written, He shall give His angels charge concerning Thee: and in their hands they shall bear Thee up, lest at any time Thou dash Thy foot against a stone.*"

IN these words is contained the brief history of Satan's second temptation of our Lord.

Now it may occur to us, brethren, to ask at once, What did man's foe desire to accomplish by this strange act and no less strange speech of his? What was the adversary aiming at? And then also it may occur to us to ask, Why should it have been any the slightest temptation to the Lord Jesus to cast Himself down from a pinnacle of the Temple? In what direction lay the strength and urgency of this special temptation? And let us approach this difficult and mysterious subject reverently, seeking the guidance of the Holy Spirit of God.

Let us bear in mind then, brethren, that Satan's object in his two first temptations would seem to have been twofold; first, to induce the Son of man to manifest Himself as the very Son of God, thus casting off poor human nature as a serpent sheds its slough; and secondly, to direct against His human nature some special temptation of the flesh or of the devil, to seek to draw Him as man from the narrow path of unswerving rectitude.

To take these things in order. It was with the object of inducing our Blessed Lord to exercise His hidden Divinity that Satan had said in the first temptation, "If Thou be the Son of God, *command* that these stones be made bread." And even so now in like manner the words of the tempter, "If Thou be the Son of God, cast Thyself down," called, it is obvious, for a manifestation of the hidden Godhead. Satan, we may be sure, as I have already indicated, would not dread any number of victories to be won by our Saviour as God, and that because the will of God is manifestly resistless. There is no contending with God. It was the Saviour's perfect righteousness as man which was calculated to confound that wicked one. For man had been created free to stand or fall, and had fallen, and man's foe would seem to have apprehended rightly that only by man, only by the promised Seed of the woman, might man be recovered from his fallen estate. And hence arose Satan's jealousy of all perfection in man, hence arose his terror, *not* of the hidden God in the Lord Jesus, but of the perfect man! So, then, the adversary would fain have had the Lord Jesus to act as God. The words "Cast Thyself down" might well signify from the lips of the tempter, Fall as if direct from the skies into the Temple courts below, among the Temple worshippers, and so ensure their homage, so compel their acclamations; and let all Jerusalem acknowledge that Thou, even Thou, coming thus suddenly to Thy Temple, art the promised Messenger, yea, even the Lord whom all men seek with ardent longing."

But next, it was no less with the object of leading the man Christ Jesus into sin that Satan plotted mischief. Manifestly it was the evil one's evil hope that our blessed Master, as man, should give way to some one impulse of evil, discontent, impatience, or even spiritual pride, and should consent to do that as the chosen favourite of heaven, which no mere man might do and live. For, as in the first temptation there had been an appeal made to the weakness of human flesh, so here there was an appeal made to the weakness of human spirit. And that was a seeming Scriptural argument which the tempter now addressed to the perfect man, truly a weak and a false argument, but sufficiently plausible to have passed muster with many. And the quoting by Satan of that particular passage of Scripture implied, "' Do not suppose that it would be presumptuous in Thee as Son of man to cast Thyself down; in any case Thou art the Elect of heaven, and of Thee "it is written, He shall give His angels charge concerning Thee: and in their hands they shall bear Thee up, lest at any time Thou dash Thy foot against a stone.'" What the devil here omitted (as we shall find on reference to the 91st Psalm) are the words "in all Thy ways," which words would appear to limit the promise of God's protection to one walking in the path of duty, and might scarcely be held to extend it to him who should wilfully strike out a path for himself. Yet I would not have it to be supposed, brethren, that our blessed Lord might not, if He pleased, thus have manifested forth His glory. There would have been nothing essentially evil or sinful in the act, any more than in walking on the waves of the sea, and, had there been, there would have been no real temptation to our Lord's pure spirit.

Truly, to have relieved hunger by turning stones into bread, and again to have vindicated His Father's glory by coming suddenly to His Temple, would have been acts strictly lawful in themselves. Why, then, did our Lord do neither of these things? Since the Lord Jesus at a later period was to perform so many miracles, as notably to walk upon the waters, why should He not now forthwith have come flying upon the wings of the wind? If the Son of man might acceptably do the one, why might He not, or at least why did He not, do the other? I answer, Because it was one thing to walk upon the waves of the sea for the confirmation of the faith of those who already believed, as of the apostles in the vessel, and another thing to cleave His way through the air in order to compel the faith of thousands, or tens and hundreds of thousands, who as yet believed not. I answer, Because it was one thing to gladden a few faithful, loving, though partially beclouded hearts, and another to dazzle the minds of a strange multitude. And on a full consideration we can see, that to have commanded the homage of the multitude by a visible descent as from heaven, would have been to make the appeal to sight, not faith. And though indeed it be most certain that the Lord Jesus did afterwards walk upon the waters, yet for all that He remained to the end, in the estimation even of those who witnessed that wonderful sight, the Son of man. But who must not see that if the Lord had consented to wing His flight through the air in the sight of the assembled multitude in the Temple courts, He would have manifested Himself unmistakably as the Son of God? as the promised Messias, who was to be discerned with the eye of faith only by willing and obedient hearts, as an act of free choice, and not of desperate necessity? And further, who does not see that to have yielded to this temptation would have been to have worked in very deed a sign from heaven, an amazing wonder, utterly unlike in character to the whole tenor of our Lord's actual miracles, which were ever wrought, so to speak, by the bye, at the immediate call of mercy, or at most for the confirmation of the faith of those who already believed?

And next, suffer me to ask, How should the evil one's suggestion have proved any real temptation to our Master Christ? Very much of mystery there must always remain in this matter, but at least it will be a true answer to say that our Lord might well feel Himself hampered and shackled by the weakness of His human nature; might well long to manifest His true but hidden Divinity, were it only for a moment; might well desire to free Himself from the tempter's presence; might well long to vindicate His Heavenly Father's glory. But still we may fail to see, brethren, how the man Christ Jesus would be tempted seriously by this temptation. Let us then remember that our Blessed Master had passed through thirty years of poverty and utter obscurity. Hence, be it said in deepest reverence, may have arisen a temptation in our Master, as man, a strong and fervent desire to come forth with the least possible delay from obscurity into practical usefulness, and accomplish His great given work.

To resume. There stood our Blessed Lord on a pinnacle of the Temple, and there stood the tempter by His side. Below were the Temple courts thronged, as we have reasonably conjectured, with worshippers. What Satan now said in effect was, "Behold the harvest! Whether Thou be the Son of God or Son of man, take the readiest means befitting Thy dignity to reap that harvest. Cast Thyself down." Every fibre of the Lord's human heart would surely beat with strongest feeling on this the occasion of His first visit to the Temple since He had been called to the public ministry. Every desire of His human heart and brain would surely be aroused to act promptly and energetically. And was the Lord bound, indeed, to refrain from taking His countrymen, so to speak, by storm as by a descent from heaven? Ay, brethren, we may venture to answer, with the light of His own reply shining upon the fact, He was so bound. Verily it would have ill become the Son of Man to perform a wonder, however glorious, in order thereby to strike awe into the minds of beholders and compel a reluctant homage to His power.

And our Lord was not to be led astray by any wresting of the Scriptures, His own Scriptures, from their true and perfect meaning. And His answer teaches us incidentally that we are to be guided by the plain precepts of God's Word, and not by any single text of doubtful purpose which it may be comparatively easy to misapply. "Jesus said unto him, It is written again, Thou shalt not tempt the Lord thy God." That is to say, Thou shalt place thyself in no needless and uncalled-for danger; thou shalt never act as if thou couldst desire to test the truth of God's promise of assistance to thee, and so encourage in others the spirit of presumption.

Thus did the Lord Jesus refuse alike to show Himself as God, or to err as man by a sin of eagerness. It was as man that the Lord Jesus made reply. It was as man that He declined in any case to tempt or seem even to tempt God. And once more Satan had to cease from his temptations with the knowledge that thus far he had been wholly baffled and defeated.

And great would now be the adversary's discomfiture. For it can hardly be said too often that what was dreaded of the devil was our Lord's victory in His human nature. Man had long been Satan's slave, and it was intolerable to the evil one that by the perfect obedience of one man a fallen world should bid fair to be reconciled to its offended Creator. Therefore again I say, the devil would either have the Lord Jesus to act as God, or else to sin a sin of presumption as man.—May it not further seem, dear brethren, as if something of the nature of a falsehood had been suggested by the adversary in his blindness to Him who was "the Truth," when he said, "Cast Thyself down"? For did not Satan hereby urge our Lord in effect to countenance the idea in men's minds that He had descended straight from heaven into the Temple courts? If so, the chief of fallen spirits did indeed desire to involve our Blessed Master in a delusion and a lie.

And now there is, I trust, conveyed to our minds some definite meaning in connexion with the second temptation of our Lord. Satan counted plainly, as one well acquainted with human nature in its weakness, that though Jesus of Nazareth had resisted a searching temptation of the flesh, He might yet yield to one more refined and spiritual, something with which the flesh was in no way concerned. And the enemy had reasonable grounds (speaking broadly) for this expectation, since it is an undoubted fact that many men who are neither gluttons nor drunkards, nor yet impure nor slothful, who, on the contrary, are remarkable for their freedom from the sins of the flesh, so called, are apt to be not a little conscious of their superiority over other men in respect of these things, and will give way, therefore, unconsciously to some degree of spiritual pride, or even sometimes, strange to say, to yet darker sins, such as hatred and falsehood. Thus men will often fall under Satan's dominion in one class of moral evil, even whilst in respect of another class the adversary may have little or no influence over them.

Let us beware of spiritual pride, brethren. Let us beware of supposing that we any of us may do certain things with safety as God's elect, which it is not given to other men to do. Let us beware of thinking that we can cast ourselves down in effect, and yet suffer no great harm, if any. Let us not tempt God by rashness, by boldness, by over-confidence. Let us walk humbly with our God. Yea, see we to it that we not only resist by God's grace the deadly temptations of the flesh, but also the far subtler temptations of the devil. And presumption, or spiritual pride, is Satan's own peculiar sin, whereby he and a third part of the heavenly host fell from heaven. Other sins which are no less Satan's very own are hatred, falsehood, blasphemy, and the tempting of others. But it is manifest that the fallen archangel, in setting his snares to catch one truly noble, must draw them as with a delicate spider's web, almost or quite invisible, and yet to the fly as adamantine. And thus he acted when seeking to ensnare the Lord Jesus Christ—so delicately indeed that, unless we look closely, the nature of the temptation may escape us altogether. With us the evil one is likely to go to work more roundly, so to speak ; but, however he may tempt us, dear brethren, let us take our Lord's example as our shield. And when the devil says to us in effect, at any time or in any manner, " Cast thyself down," let us bear in mind the sovereign precept, " Thou shalt not tempt the Lord thy God," and answer him therewith. Though Satan is strong, a Stronger than he fights for us. God is on our side, even Father, Son, and Holy Ghost. He can preserve us, though Satan should catch us up as it were to a giddy height, and, under one specious pretext or another, bid us seek our own ruin. The devil cannot cast you down, brethren. He is powerless to achieve your destruction. Only you yourselves can cast down yourselves. But take your stand with Christ your Master, and place your trust in the warning and guidance of God's Holy Word. So shall the blessed Spirit guard you from Satan's utmost malice for ever and for ever.

III.

THE THIRD TEMPTATION, TO A GRASPING UNDULY AT THE WORLD'S SALVATION.

THE THIRD TEMPTATION, TO A GRASPING UNDULY AT THE WORLD'S SALVATION.

S. Matthew iv. 8, 9.

"Again, the devil taketh Him up into an exceeding high mountain, and showeth Him all the kingdoms of the world, and the glory of them; and saith unto Him, All these things will I give Thee, if Thou wilt fall down and worship me."

HAVING assailed the Son of Man in succession with a temptation of the flesh and of the devil, the great adversary next and last assailed Him with a temptation of the world; yet not a temptation of the world only, but this would seem the more prominent aspect of the third trial. In vain had Satan bidden the Son of man command stones to be made bread for His own use. In vain had he bidden Him cast Himself down in spiritual pride as the favourite of heaven, so tempting God. Should it now prove equally vain to offer to Him all the kingdoms of the world? That remained to be seen. This time at least the temptation should not be wanting in strength, in breadth, in seeming majesty. What an offer! all the kingdoms of the world! Of what baseness will not too many men be guilty to gain some petty worldly advantage! What a bewildering thought is the attainment of a single throne! And who, then, might not be dazzled by the offer of the whole world?

It is remarkable that man's foe no longer says this time, as twice he had said before, "If Thou be the Son of God." The third and last temptation would seem to have been addressed to the man Christ Jesus exclusively, and not in any sense to have been a challenge to the hidden God to show Himself. That is to say, apparently, no third attempt was made to induce the Son of man to act as the Son of God, whether to create food, or to fly through the air, or otherwise to manifest Deity. All *that* was over and past. And now the Lord Jesus was simply tempted to reign as man over all earth's kingdoms. He was not tempted to seize on those kingdoms as Son of God by His own might, but to accept them as Son of man as a gift, on one seemingly slight condition.

Possibly the steadfast answers which the Lord Jesus had given in the character of man to the former temptations, holding Himself each time bound by the written word, and declining to do any thing which it did not become a man to do, had almost persuaded Satan that after all he had to deal with a man only—but that man a perfect man. If so, this would be far indeed from reassuring the adversary, who, as we scarcely need to be reminded, dreaded not what God might do—since God was altogether above him and away—but *did* dread exceedingly lest a second man should stand where the first man, Adam, had fallen, and so by a life and death of perfect obedience should reconcile a fallen world to the Father. Therefore it behoved the fallen archangel by all the means within his power to move this man from His perfect righteousness. And whether the enemy still suspected a union of the Godhead with the manhood in the Lord Jesus or not, *this* at least he failed not to perceive, that he had to deal with a perfect man, and that by some means he must make this man, if it were possible, swerve from the straight path. No bid could be too high to secure this needful triumph. And clearly the sin proposed or suggested must seem so slight, as hardly to appear a sin, if it were to have any chance whatever of prevailing.

Now, brethren, let us come to the facts. From the

mountain height, to which the chief of fallen spirits had conveyed the Saviour, might be seen with the natural eye, not indeed the whole world as it is known to us, but the foremost countries of the then known world; and if not all the countries themselves, at least that famous sea, the Mediterranean, which washed all their shores. But it is not for us to limit what the Saviour would see on this occasion to that which it would be given to us to behold from the very same mountain height. Where all was miracle, it is not for us to stand questioning and balancing nicely as to whether they were ten or twenty countries, or a hundred or a thousand, which were more or less unfolded as by vision to the view of the Son of man. Enough that it is written, "The devil taketh Him up into an exceeding high mountain, and showeth Him all the kingdoms of the world, and the glory of them." Thus far S. Matthew. And S. Luke adds the words, "In a moment of time,"—so calling attention to the miraculous character of the vision. And those words of S. Matthew, "and the glory of them," imply more—far more—than the mere glimmering through the haze of the bare outline of this or that distant land, imply more, also, than the clearest oversight of their hills and valleys, and fruitful plains, and proud cities;

imply, in truth, nothing less than that to our Lord as He gazed would be opened out all the glories, past, present, and future, of those countries—glories of art, science, earthly knowledge—glories of mind as well as all material splendours. And thus would the temptation to rule over the whole world gain in force. Thus also might ambition—a noble and a grand ambition—to rule and guide those countries, yea, humanity at large, for God's glory, be the more easily aroused in our Lord's human breast.

And Satan, not appearing, be it borne in mind, as the fallen spirit of darkness (for then temptation there could have been none), but rather as an angel of light and glory (as it is written, "Satan himself is transformed into an angel of light"), made offer of all these kingdoms, of all this majesty, to the Son of man. He offered all this magnificence—nay, more, all this boundless opportunity for good upon the vastest scale —to Jesus of Nazareth, to Him who had been bred up amid poverty and obscurity for thirty years in a mountain village. Say, dear brethren, was it not, from a human point of view at least, a most dazzling offer? And be it noted that hell's lord did not offer all earth's kingdoms as from himself. No, he represented himself, so S. Luke tells us, as having authority from another (and that other who but God?) to dispose absolutely of the power and glory of this world, saying, "For that is *delivered* unto me, and to whomsoever I will I give it." And whether the adversary spoke falsely or truly, the temptation might, and probably would be the same to the man Christ Jesus. In either case the temptation would be real. That it is most essential to note and to believe. Remember that the seeming angel of light who thus tempted our Blessed Master had given signal proof of his power in transporting the Son of man to the mountain height, and in showing Him all earth's kingdoms in a moment of time. And say, was there any reason why his offer should not appear real? No, surely, there was not any. And doubtless as real, most real, the Son of man would entertain it.

But, further, the tempter attached one condition to his splendid offer. That condition ran as follows: "All these things will I give Thee, if Thou wilt fall down and worship me." At first sight this may seem to us a monstrous demand, for is not worship God's prerogative? but doubtless it was a mere passing act of homage and of secondary worship which was here claimed. And, again be it said, we may not think that Satan claimed this act of homage as the adversary, else would he certainly and most foolishly have defeated his own object. For who but the most desperate of mankind would knowingly and with open eyes pay an act of homage to the chief of fallen spirits? So, then, although our Lord's answer presently teaches us that He, in truth, discerned who and what the tempter was, yet that tempter himself would gladly have continued to appear in the light of some glorious angel or archangel, and actually did assume that very character. And we can all see that it could have been no gross or monstrous sin into which the tempter could hope to precipitate the perfect man, but rather such an error as should appear hardly a sin at all. And to a noble mind off its guard it might truly seem a small matter to bow the knee for an instant to a good angel, an angel of light and glory, as the condition of being placed in a position to pour the greatest blessings upon mankind. Nay, we know that S. John, the beloved disciple, did this without any entreaty—did this even after having been forbidden, as an involuntary act of loving reverence. He fell at an angel's feet to worship him, to gain no special end, by a mere instinct of devotion (Rev. xxii. 8). Why should not Jesus of Nazareth do as much to gain and possibly to save the whole world, to spread abroad all knowledge of His Heavenly Father, to bind all nations by one common law of trust and love, to hasten the deliverance of mankind from the thraldom of sin and woe?

But the man Christ Jesus would not accept the gift now offered to Him; and, least of all, would He accept it at such a price.

First, I say, He desired not the gift of the world's glories for Himself. He the Son of man desired not with His higher will to grasp at grand and hasty results. Rather, we may be sure, would He willingly work upward and onward from small beginnings. Rather would He at the outset gather His Apostles around Him, and next win single souls painfully and slowly, but surely. Rather would He sow the seeds of life eternal in men's hearts amidst sorrow and partial failure. He came not to command but to persuade. Far from Him would be the resolve to run a brilliant and a resistless career of triumph. "It behoved Christ to suffer," if He was to move the great heart of the world. And was it not His one fixed purpose to suffer willingly whatever of suffering it might please His Heavenly Father to inflict upon Him? Ay, truly was it so. And should He forsake that lowly obedience which was so dear to the Father's heart, and in the stead thereof rule as monarch over the kingdoms of the world? This was not a thought to be seriously entertained! And yet, brethren, see the workings of this great temptation! Might not the nations be brought far more speedily and triumphantly into the Gospel net by the method thus proposed than by that which had originated in the councils of the everlasting Godhead? Might not whole nations be converted from heathenism in a day, in an hour, whom else it should take thousands of years to convert? For who should resist the will of an universal earthly monarch? Who should so much as desire to thwart him? Might this be by possibility a heavenly suggestion, even an afterthought of heaven? Remember, brethren, I repeat, the temptation was real. But for the temptation to be real, our Blessed Lord's pure human nature must have been tried apart from His Divinity. We may not bring in omniscience or divine knowledge, for that would be to render all a make-believe, an unreality. We must with all reverence assume that our Blessed Lord did not clearly know, could not have fully known at this instant of time, how God's will was to be accomplished. What He did doubtless see was a boundless present good to be achieved at the cost of a seemingly very slight deviation from the perfectly right path, a single momentary act of secondary worship to one who claimed to be an angel of God, and who was permitted by God to exercise a mighty sovereignty, "For this is delivered unto me." And yet, what should it profit the Son of man to gain millions of facile, easily-moulded converts, dazzled and not truly persuaded? And where then would be the glorious example for mankind of a patient obedience unto death? Where also would be the lessons of a perfect life of lowliness? Where, in a word, would be the teaching of the Cross? No, the Son of man would not really accept such a gift as the tempter had it in his power to bestow. Results should not be grasped at. The lowly birth in Bethlehem, and the thirty years of poverty in Nazareth, should not be exchanged for a sudden, earthly glory. Rather should the three remaining years of suffering and the closing death of shame be endured bravely by Him who knew so well how to set His face as a flint, but who suffered not, remember, the less acutely, the less intensely, in so doing.

But, as for the condition attached to the offer of the gift, *that* revealed the fiend. For this thing was forbidden, even all secondary worship whatsoever. And he could be no good angel who claimed even one moment's reverential homage or secondary worship. And, accordingly, the man Christ Jesus, keeping terms no longer with the tempter, as hitherto He had in a manner borne with him, now finally broke out into just indignation, crying, "Get thee hence, Satan!" Yea, Satan, the adversary! Seen to be such by pure human penetration, despite of all attempts at concealment. "Get thee hence, Satan: for it is written, Thou shalt worship the Lord thy God, and Him only shalt thou serve." O dear brethren, that we all had a share in our Lord's impassioned outbreak on this theme! O for some little measure of our Lord's just indignation against the tempter when we are in any wise thus tempted! O for some zeal for God's especial honour! O for the honest and good heart which sees through the tempter's devices, and rejects them with horror and dismay. When Satan tempted our Lord he desired nothing less than to overthrow the mighty plan of redemption. And when Satan tempts us he desires to defeat God's gracious purpose of salvation on our behalf, he desires to ruin our souls. O that we might say in our turn, when tempted to grasp unduly at results of whatsoever kind, when tempted to forsake the path of duty for that of inclination, when tempted to make some slight concession to that which is forbidden, in order to become rich or successful in life, or even to attain a good and righteous or a holy end,—"Get thee behind me, Satan!" Would that we too might fall back on Holy Scripture, on eternal right, and say, "It is written, Thou shalt worship the Lord thy God, and Him only shalt thou serve."

Here, brethren, I will not pause to glance at the actual temptation to secondary worship, to the worship of angels or of departed saints in this day, urged for the sake of charity, or in order to promote the reunion of Christendom and the consequent benefit of the Church Catholic and glory of God. But this is a subtle snare spread mainly for the masters in Israel. Our lesson is plain. To all suggestions of wrong-doing in however small a way, in order to attain what seems a good, or useful, or a blessed and holy end, let us turn a deaf ear, or rather answer resolutely, "Get thee behind me, Satan."

And thus the last and greatest of the adversary's temptations failed to gain a hold on the perfect man, even as the sea spray is dashed from off a rock,—and the glorious work of redemption went forward in a lowly obedience unto the end. It is difficult, brethren, to speak at all worthily of the three temptations of our Blessed Master which have now, one at a time, been brought under your notice. There are mysteries in them, as affecting the Son of man who was also the Son of God, which it may hardly be given to us to fathom. But at least this is made plain, that our three deadly foes are the world, the flesh, and the devil.

These are the things which you young people (who are looking forward here to Confirmation) have to renounce. Oh, renounce them with all your hearts. And let us shun the beginnings of evil, whatever fair semblance these may by the tempter's device be made to bear. Never may we do even the least evil that good may come of it, as, for instance, by telling what may seem expedient falsehoods and the like. And in time of temptation let us turn for help in prayer to God, and have recourse to His Word. Then shall the devil leave us as he left our Saviour; then also shall the angels come and minister to us, even as they " came and ministered unto Him." Finally, let us be certain that in all our temptations we have our Great Master's sympathy. He knows what it is to be tempted, and He feels for us. "We have not an high priest which cannot be touched with the feeling of our infirmities." Let this thought strengthen us in all our trials. Let us remember that it is written again, "For in that He Himself hath suffered, being tempted, He is able to succour them that are tempted." Let us open our hearts to our Lord's loving warning, prompted it may be in some measure by the recollection of the third and last of His own temptations, "What shall it profit a man if he shall gain the whole world, and lose his own soul? Or what shall a man give in exchange for his soul?"

The Obedience unto Death.

"*In burnt offerings and sacrifices for sin Thou hast had no pleasure. Then said I, Lo, I come . . . to do Thy will, O God.*"

INTRODUCTION.

IF that has been high which hitherto has formed the argument of this volume, verily that which follows is higher yet. For where shall we find greater depth, and height, and breadth, than in the obedience unto death, even the death of the Cross, of the Son of the Father? Those who read, will they bear in mind that the glorious theme involves necessarily much of seeming daring? Will they bear in mind that he who would speak with open heart of the Almighty Father's sympathy with the Only-begotten Son, of the Holy Spirit's coequal share in the work of redemption, must leave perforce the shore, must, as it were, sail forth into mid-ocean? There ships founder. There also ships by God's hand are preserved, and discharge their appointed mission. Man is free to brave the perils of the ocean. And who can question that the mightier ocean of God's redeeming love may also lawfully be sailed forth upon by the Christian in a spirit of deepest reverence and lowly faith? Such a spirit has been here aimed at. But the greatness of the theme cannot but appal, even whilst it inspires. The attitude of mind in which to approach the subject of the obedience unto death may be summed up best perhaps in Christendom's ancient ascription of praise: Glory be to the Father, and to the Son, and to the Holy Ghost: as it was in the beginning, is now, and ever shall be, world without end. Amen.

I.
THE FATHER'S LOVE.

THE FATHER'S LOVE.

Genesis xxii. 8.

"And Abraham said, My son, God will provide Himself a Lamb for a burnt offering."

WE can hardly approach the record of Abraham's matchless faith, in consenting to sacrifice his son Isaac, without a feeling of awe, instinctively conscious as we must be that therein we may trace, as "through a glass darkly," heavenly, and all but unspeakable mysteries. And indeed the whole story, deeply interesting as it is in its plain and literal meaning, is also a mighty parable in which Abraham may be plainly said to represent the Almighty Father, while Isaac, the willing sacrifice, fills the place of no other than our Blessed Lord. In very truth, the scene on Mount Moriah is a distinct and amazing type or foreshadowing of the awful transaction on Mount Calvary.

And now to turn to my inspiring task. Abraham, we know, was rich in flocks and in herds; and doubtless he would have taken gladly thrice a hundred lambs or kids from the fold, so that there should have been no lack of burnt offerings, if only thereby he might have spared one slightest ill to his well-beloved son, Isaac. Nay more, we may not doubt that, to save his son, Abraham would willingly have laid down his own life. But neither of these things might be. The voice of God, well known to Abraham, had spoken. The unmistakable command was ringing in his ears, "Take now thy son, thine only son Isaac, whom thou lovest, and get thee into the land of Moriah; and offer him there for a burnt offering upon one of the mountains which I will tell thee of." O blackness of thick darkness! his only son claimed by the Lord as a burnt offering! It may almost have seemed, but for its dread reality, like a bad and monstrous dream.

Well may each generation of believers ask in turn, How could a loving father endure so fierce a trial? And we the living Christians of this day have a right to ask, Can Abraham's consent be accounted for in a way that shall satisfy the human heart at its best and noblest? Listen, beloved, and let your own hearts be the judge.

Abraham, be it then remembered, knew God's great goodness of old. Till now he had ever found the voice of God a voice of blessing. He would therefore feel it to be impossible, literally impossible, that the Lord should command him to slay his son—and that *there* should be an end! For even setting aside all the glorious promises already made to him through that son, it might well appear that his God would be incapable of such an act. Faith and love forbade this conclusion. Let God's command appear never so cruel, it must be so in seeming only. And yet truly what faith was needed to reason thus justly before the event—what faith, what absolute trust! Abraham indeed, I repeat, was no stranger to God's great goodness. Had not the patriarch been blessed throughout a long life by the Lord's fatherly care and tender guidance? Had not he pleaded fearlessly face to face with the Lord, as to a merciful Creator, for Sodom the guilty city? And had he not so far prevailed with the Lord, that if only ten righteous men had been found therein it had been spared? So then, I say once more, Abraham was well assured that the Lord was a God of mercy; he was intimately persuaded in his heart of hearts of God's goodness, so that he might have cried out with Job, "Though He slay me, yet will I trust Him." And this perfect trust, this simple faith in the goodness of God, it was which carried Abraham safely through his tremendous ordeal. Further, one plain hope which Abraham cherished has been revealed to us in the Epistle to the Hebrews (xi. 17) where it is written, "By faith Abraham, when he was tried, offered up Isaac . . . accounting that God was able to raise him up, even from the dead; from whence also he received him in a figure." But let it suffice to say, my brethren, that the strong and simple faith of Abraham rested above all things on his intimate persuasion of God's goodness. And, I ask, may *that* satisfy our hearts or not? Have we yet to seek far and wide for some further reasons why we may acquit Abraham of acquiescence in seeming evil? Or is the noblest of all reasons for his obedience already found? Verily our faith and trust as Christians rest on no other foundation.

So then, brethren, with Abraham to hear was to obey. Accompanied by Isaac, and attended by two of his young men, he set out. Some few words the patriarch spoke to these young men, which at once serve to show that hope had not deserted him: "I and the lad will go yonder and worship, and come again to you;" *and come again to you!* But Abraham was to speak more hopeful words than these when Isaac presently should ask that most thrilling question, "My father ... Behold the fire and the wood: but where is the lamb for a burnt offering?" Then in the patriarch's answer we may see, as it were, the very point to which his hopes were turned. "And Abraham said, My son, God will provide Himself a Lamb for a burnt offering." Surely when the patriarch spoke these touching words, there was no wish to deceive, for soon the mountain top would be reached where all must be revealed. Rather may it appear that, inspired by the intensity of his sacred sorrow, Abraham gave utterance, consciously or unconsciously, to a prophecy, which lifted, it may be, for an instant, the great burden from off his own heart, even whilst it should bring comfort to all future generations. Verily Abraham prophesied in the letter that the Lamb of God, and none but He, should prove an acceptable sacrifice. And thus also he expressed his trust, his unwavering trust in God. And then for the further and complete trial of his faith, the prophetic spirit probably left him. And in silent awe father and son would ascend the mountain-side together, Isaac bearing the wood on which he was to be stretched on the summit of the mountain.—Even thus beloved brethren, Jesus our Lord should later ascend, according to Christendom's common belief, the selfsame sacred hill, even Calvary, bearing the cross on which He was to endure the burden of the sins of the world. Let your hearts here note that Abraham advanced lovingly and pityingly step by step beside his patient, trustful son, nor ever left him. And now to lift up your minds to a far holier, a far more surpassing vision, and to come away from the narrative, or seek rather at once for its full prophetic significance, remember, yes, remember, that even thus the Eternal Father companied with our dear Master Christ along the way of sorrows. And though the Father's countenance was hidden for three mortal hours from the beloved Son upon the cross of Calvary, when the amazing cry went up, "My God, My God, why hast Thou forsaken Me?" when thick darkness covered the earth—yet even then, yea, then even above all (dare we doubt it?) was the Father's ·pitying gaze bent in unspeakable love upon His own afflicted Son.

Yes, brethren, in the grief of Abraham we may behold a faint picture of the compassion of the eternal Father! And if you pity the creature, I would say, love, love from the very depths of your soul, with silent awe, with unspeakable wonder, with deep yearning of heart, the great Creator, even whilst you adore His sovereign goodness.

We know the Lamb of God. We know in whom we have believed. We know Him who is tender, infinitely mild and gracious, absolutely generous and true. But do we know the Father? Ah, do we know the Father? Have we ever faintly realized the sacrifice which it must needs have cost the almighty Father's heart to render up the Lamb whom He provided for an offering to Himself?

This may seem too daring a question to propose. We are told that God has not parts or passions; but Holy Scripture tells us that God was grieved at the heart again and yet again, and I am content to use the words of Scripture, knowing that no human words can perfectly express divine things. But I am jealous, brethren, I venture to be jealous, for the love due to our heavenly Father. I fear some of us do not feel that, and take for granted His part in the work of our redemption, and do not understand that He gave His Only-beloved Son, and that, as far as Deity is capable of loss, that gift must have involved a marvellous, an unspeakable self-sacrifice. If it cost the everlasting Son much to become man, to suffer, and to die, did it cost the almighty Father nothing to witness and accept that wonderful Sacrifice of sacrifices? And must we not love the Father as we love the Son?

Suffer me, then, to pursue this awful, this wonderful, this most glorious theme; and may God's Holy Spirit guard me from a forbidden or an irreverent thought or expression! I am pleading for the love due to our heavenly Father, and love only commands love; therefore must I show you, brethren, or seek to show you, the heavenly Father's love for us His creatures. When I speak of divine grief, vexation or sorrow, I use strictly Scriptural language, and would desire to be understood only in a guarded and a Scriptural sense. And with this caution I proceed.

Even Abraham's grief of heart then, when he looked forward to the sacrifice of his son Isaac by his own hand, amid no insults and no profanations, is almost too painful to contemplate in spite of the happy ending. Therefore may we well shrink, beloved brethren, from too close a scrutiny into that other, that infinitely greater and more amazing sacrifice of which I speak. That is indeed inexpressibly sacred, yea, it is most awful ground. Yet may we reverently acknowledge our debt of boundless gratitude to our almighty Father. Yet may we seek to apprehend something of His most marvellous goodness.

And now to proceed another step in the sacred narrative, in the mighty parable before us. To the earthly father and the earthly son comfort was sent. Those words, "The Lord will provide Himself a Lamb for a burnt offering," had come to them both like a ray of sunshine in the deepest gloom, recalling the power and infinite mercy of the Lord, nor did they hold out a vain hope. The ram caught in the thicket was provided, and so Isaac was saved. But it was otherwise, it was far otherwise, beloved brethren, with the heavenly Father and the Only-begotten Son. There, there—the cup should not be taken away. In that consummate work of redemption nothing was allowed to come between the will and the deed; no other lamb should be provided. God did not spare His own Son as He spared the child of Abraham, but suffered Him to lay down His life upon the cross, and love, infinite love, prompted the unbounded sacrifice.

And here a thoughtful and a reverent heart may dare to ask, if we are tempted to feel dismay at the thought of Abraham lifting up his hand against his son Isaac, why are we resigned to the thought of God the Father's consent being given to the death of His only Son as man? Let me answer, let me venture to reply in all humility, deeply moved we ought to be indeed, yea, and utterly melted by the knowledge of the Divine Sacrifice, but in no sense dismayed because the will of Father and of Son, yea, of Father, Son, and Spirit, was at one, as could not be the wills of Abraham and of Isaac; because whereas the sacrifice of Isaac would have been at best but a touching act of faith and trust, without other motive than a blind obedience, leading to no apparent good—the sacrifice of the Son of God was a conscious and intelligent offering made by most infinite love, a willing obedience unto death, even the death of the cross, a most mighty and sufficient remedy for an almost boundless evil, the appointed dispensation for the raising of a fallen world. Further, brethren, we do not think it contrary, but rather according to right that the parents should, if need arise, sacrifice themselves for the children, and if the earthly parents for the earthly children, then also why not,—let me dare to say the word, dread and tremendous as it may appear—why not the Father of all for all His children here?

The work of atonement, let us clearly apprehend, beloved, is of the Father and of the Spirit as well as of the Son. Nor was it the sufferings of His beloved Son in themselves alone—need I say?—which reconciled the Father to a sinful world, but rather that unfailing, that consummate obedience, perfected by anguish unto death, of which the sufferings were the proof and trial, and also the glory and the crown. For these and manifold reasons (reasons which I need not pause to dwell on now) we are not surprised that God's love should shrink from no sacrifice, that our great Master's obedience should not stay short of death, but are able to hear with joy and wonder-stricken gratitude that Jesus died for our sins upon the cross, and that the Father and the Spirit gave consent.

Ay, the Holy Spirit! no less than the Father and the Son. For that grace which prevailed in Abraham over possible rebellion and despair, that grace also which prevailed in Isaac over possible disobedience and refusal to die when the full horror of Mount Moriah burst upon his view,—what was it truly but the influence of God the Holy Spirit ! The Holy Spirit we may be sure was with Abraham and with Isaac. And we know that He the glorious Spirit was and is One with the Almighty Father and the Everlasting Son. The Holy Spirit inspired the obedience unto death of Isaac, and dwelt without measure in Isaac's and the world's Redeemer. In the councils of the thrice Holy Trinity in Unity the Lamb was slain from all eternity, and thus may we boldly say, as far as language can express what is unutterable, that the Holy Spirit companied with the Father and with the Son upon Mount Calvary, and shared in the fathomless woe and in the divine joy and boundless glory of the great work of redemption.

It does not enter into my design, brethren, to tell the patriarchal story further at this time. We know the suspense which followed on Mount Moriah, and the happy ending, already glanced at indeed, how the ram caught in the thicket was offered up for a burnt offering in the stead of Isaac, how the greatest of blessings was pronounced from heaven upon Abraham, how it was foretold that in him all the nations of the earth should be blessed.

But now to drop what is almost too deep and holy for all human thought, and far more for human expression, would that the history of Abraham's faith might strengthen in our hearts the spirit of simple trust!

Never indeed, need I say, can there befall us a trial in all respects so severe, so terrible, as that which befell Abraham. God's commands and the promptings of natural affection are for us one and the same thing, not seemingly opposed. It is not possible, I mean, that we should be called upon to sacrifice literally to the Lord our flesh and blood, though the call may still reach us to suffer our sons and daughters to venture their lives in God's service,—say in missionary labours, or in nursing the sick, or on the battlefield. And so we need never be tempted to despair of God and goodness to the like fearful extent that Abraham was tempted. And yet no doubt our faith may be proved by desolating trials, by what may seem painful or even torturing doubts,—almost more than we can bear. Then it is, dear brethren, at such times, when it may be we see our very means of existence imperilled, or when God takes to Himself by death those we most dearly love, when God's providence seems most dark and inscrutable,—*then it is* that Abraham's example may encourage us to trust in the Lord, to say in our hearts, " He is good ;" to trust in Him let come what may ; to call to mind our beloved Master's words, "Whosoever shall lose his life shall preserve it;" to rest on the assurance, "God is Love."

For if Abraham had cause to trust God, surely we have immeasurably greater cause. We can say not only God *will* provide, but God *has* provided Himself a Lamb for a burnt offering. Nearly nineteen centuries have rolled away since the Lord provided unto Himself that Lamb concerning whom Abraham prophesied. And Jesus is that Lamb.

So then without Jesus the Lamb of God we had been blind to God's love. In and through Him, by faith in Him, we are saved. A death more terrible than that which threatened Isaac on Mount Moriah, even everlasting death, the death of coldness, selfishness, and sin, would have overtaken us if Jesus had not been obedient unto death for our sakes. He is the ram caught willingly in the thicket, who was sacrificed once for all in our stead. Surely some gratitude, some gladness, for so great salvation befits us. When Abraham returned to Sarah his wife with Isaac safe beside him, must not his heart have overflowed with joy? Must not his faith in God's goodness, strong before, have been increased a thousandfold? And shall we not thank God for His inestimable love in the redemption of the world by our Lord Jesus Christ? Shall not we thank Him for the hope of glory? Yea, humbly, lovingly, trustfully, let us render back to the Almighty His own blessing bestowed on Abraham, and even dare to say, "Because Thou hast done this thing, and hast not withheld Thy Son, Thine only Son" —therefore we worship and glorify Thy name, world without end: yea, we praise Thee, we worship Thee, we glorify Thee, we give thanks to Thee for Thy great glory.

II.
THE ATONEMENT.

THE ATONEMENT.

Hebrews ix. 12.

"*Neither by the blood of goats and calves, but by His own blood He entered in once into the holy place, having obtained eternal redemption for us.*"

IT is not easy, brethren, to do justice to the Epistle to the Hebrews. It spoke clearly to the Israelite acquainted with sin-offerings all his life long, acquainted also with each minutest circumstance of the Temple worship in Jerusalem; but to us, who have never seen any blood-offerings, or sin-offerings, who hardly realize what they were, and who for the more part have but a vague conception of what constituted the essence of the Temple worship, namely, the sacrifice and offering of dumb creatures, that Epistle may be said to speak comparatively a strange language. The Apostle was arguing in it with Jews who had become Christians, and were in danger of apostatizing back to Judaism again; he was pointing out to them how the sin-offerings of the Temple were done away, how the offering of the precious blood of Jesus had taken their place; and to the born and bred Jew at that time every illustration used would be familiar. The main subject, then, of the Epistle to the Hebrews is one with which we Christians from among the Gentiles can have no practical familiarity. But in spite of that I am persuaded that a Christian congregation need not fail to enter into the meaning of the text, or indeed of the whole glorious Epistle from which it is taken, when that meaning is plainly and carefully set forth. And the result of each honest endeavour to open out to Christian hearts the great Epistle to the Hebrews in its sacrificial aspect should be a better understanding of the mighty mystery of the Atonement.

And first, then, for our guidance in this matter, let me remind you very briefly, that daily, at sunrise and at sunset, a lamb was sacrificed within the Temple bounds in Jerusalem. This was the daily offering of the Jewish Church, and may with justice be said to have formed the principal feature in the Temple worship. Now, without aiming at minute exactness, it may suffice to state that the priests slew the lamb as a so-called sin-offering; and next they offered it as a so-called burnt-offering to be consumed by fire. In the Temple itself, or actual building, were two divisions, called respectively the first and second tabernacles, into the first of which "the priests went always, accomplishing the service of God." "But into the second (which is called the holiest of all) went the high priest alone once every year, not without blood, which he offered for himself, and for the errors of the people."

So then, my brethren, you will remark that in the text a distinction is drawn between the blood of Christ and the blood of beasts, between the countless sacrifices of the Law and the one prevailing sacrifice of the Lamb of God. And in the text a further distinction is drawn between the Jewish high priest entering "once every year not without blood" into the so-called "holiest of all," or innermost sanctuary of the Temple, and our Lord's single entrance, never to be repeated, as it is written, "He entered in once into the holy place," that is, into heaven: "for Christ is not entered into the holy places made with hands, which are the figures of the true; but into heaven itself, now to appear in the presence of God for us."

How much more precious the blood of Christ is than the blood of any innocent dumb beast needs not to be insisted on, since we know that man is of "more value than many sparrows." But that the blood of Jesus Christ should be so exceedingly precious, so infinitely more precious than that of all other men may demand careful explanation. We know then that the blood of the saints is precious in God's sight, as it is written in the 72nd Psalm, "And dear (or precious) shall their blood be in His sight." But the blood of Christ alone is spoken of emphatically as "the precious blood." And why is this? It is (to give one great and indeed manifest reason,) because Christ alone is without sin, because the blood of Christ and none beside was "as that of a lamb without blemish and without spot;" and to state at once the chiefest of all reasons, it is because the Godhead was and is united to the manhood in Christ our Master, and this union lent of necessity an infinite value to that most sacred blood. But what is meant by blood? and what is meant by the offering of blood? This is worthy of our most thoughtful consideration.

Suffer me, then, my brethren, to call your attention to the statement in the book of Leviticus, at the 17th chapter and the 11th verse, "For it is *the blood* that maketh an atonement for the soul." How should that ghastly thing, it may be asked, at the sight of which strong men are apt to shrink, red blood, "the life of the flesh"—how should this make an atonement for the soul? How should the shedding of blood, either of beast or man, obtain God's pardon or remission of sins? Can it possibly be laid down as a principle (as the enemies of the Gospel sometimes have tauntingly affirmed) that God can only be appeased, can only be moved to forgiveness, by the shedding of blood? Oh no, God forbid! Yet such was undoubtedly the regulation of the Law of Moses, as we read, "And almost all things are *by the law* purged with blood; and without shedding of blood is no remission" (Heb. ix. 22), that is, under the Law. Now, that there was some good reason for this very terrible arrangement under the Law, independent of its own intrinsic value, is what we are driven to take for granted, when in the Epistle to the Hebrews (x. 4) we read the inspired utterance, "For it is not possible that the blood of bulls and of goats should take away sins," when also we take into account the horror of bloodshed which elsewhere is so freely expressed on the part of Almighty God. For it is certain that God has no delight in blood, or even in any offering of blood, *in itself*. And so He certifies by the mouth of His prophet Isaiah, saying, "I delight not in the blood of bullocks, or of lambs, or of he-goats" (i. 11). So likewise He certifies by the mouth of David, saying, "Thinkest thou that I will eat bulls' flesh, and drink the blood of goats?" (Ps. l. 13.) God was even wearied by the many sacrifices of His people Israel, sacrifices to which they attached no true meaning or import; and so Isaiah cries out (i. 11), "To what purpose is the multitude of your sacrifices unto Me? saith the Lord." But though God asked this question of the Jews by His prophet, yet, as has been said, nothing is more certain than that sacrifices and blood or sin-offerings were by Him commanded, were an essential part of the Jewish Law. Now then I ask again, why were these things commanded, seeing that in themselves they availed not to "take away sins"? seeing also that God delighteth not in blood? Surely, the reason, the excellent and abundant reason, is manifest,— even that they might serve to point onward to Christ our Lord, offering His own most precious blood upon the cross of Calvary. And accordingly, to Him, to the Saviour, the sacrifices which were under the Law,— both blood-offerings and burnt-offerings—did most assuredly point forward as to some mighty, and mysterious, and all-prevailing Sacrifice to come! By their means Christ crucified was preached in a figure to many generations, and the Atonement was constantly foreshadowed, and by a type proclaimed. Again and again was the lesson taught, not in mere words, but by a most striking sign, by an open shedding of blood, that the innocent should in some sense be sacrificed for the guilty, even as the innocent dumb beasts were slain for guilty men. And thus was the attention of the faithful Israelite called to the Lamb of God, which should lay down His life for the sins of the world. Thus also are we Christians confirmed in our belief in the prevailing power of the Atonement.

And if the thought should here cross any mind, How could God sanction the infliction of pain upon His innocent dumb creatures? it may suffice to answer that actual pain there would be little or none in what was really an almost instantaneous death,—whilst from the anticipation of pain and death, which forms man's worst trial, the dumb creation is by God's providence wholly shielded.

But to return to our wider theme. If, as is most sure, it be a delusion to imagine that God can only be appeased by blood,—if, in itself, the shedding of blood be even distasteful and repugnant to a merciful Creator,—then may this further question naturally arise, Why should the Saviour's blood have such marvellous power with God? such amazing and subduing power as to make atonement for a fallen world? as it is written, "The blood of Jesus Christ His Son cleanseth us from all sin" (1 John i. 7). Plainly, my dear brethren; and here I invite your attention to a mighty Gospel truth, because the shedding of our Saviour's blood was the expression and the sign of His voluntary obedience, His obedience unto death. That voluntary perfect fulfilment of the whole law of God, under bitterest trials and unto death, it was, emphatically, which was so acceptable, so delightful, so capable of satisfying the mind of God. And so it is written, "In burnt offerings and sacrifices for sin Thou hast had no pleasure. Then said I, Lo, I come (in the volume of the book it is written of Me) *to do Thy will*, O God." This, then, beloved brethren, is what the Saviour came to *do*. He came to do God's holy will perfectly and unto the end; and because that generation to which He came was most perverse, therefore in so doing He necessarily "resisted unto blood." I do not mean to say that there is not a deep mystery involved in the voluntary endurance of intensest anguish. On the contrary, these two great things combine to satisfy the mind of God, a spotless righteousness, and a love proved by unspeakable humiliation and altogether soundless anguish of soul; and of that marvellous all-prevailing passion, blood, the shedding of blood, is the external sign and character. But you will perceive, it is not the blood in itself, but it is the blood as the outward token of a finished obedience unto death, and as the evidence of the voluntary endurance of boundless humiliation and anguish, which has such infinite value in the sight of God.

It is, therefore, scarcely too much to say, though here we must tread most cautiously, that had the Jews not willed to put the Messiah to death, Deity might have accepted His perfect obedience and entire submission, and still boundless humiliation, as being a true and sufficient atonement for the sins of the world, and *that* even without any shedding of blood. But this is, of a truth, in one sense, a needless speculation, because the sin and obstinacy of the Jewish people were foreseen, and the Lamb was slain in God's councils from the beginning, and before time was. And indeed we can scarcely picture to ourselves any other than a crucified Redeemer. For how, except the Son of man had been thus lifted up, should God's tremendous anger against sin and evil have been made apparent to the world as now it is made apparent? And at the least it is certain, as I have said, that the blessed, glorious Trinity gave consent to the death of the of man upon the cross long, long before the malice of the Jews had been aroused; yea, so early as in the garden of Eden, yea, even before man was created, as in the book of Revelation we read plainly of " the Lamb slain from the foundation of the world." The Jews, indeed, were free to accept or to reject the true Messiah; but, forasmuch as God knows all things, the end was by Him foreseen from the beginning. And therefore the sacrifices of the Law of Moses were shaped in exact accordance with the future known to God; therefore dumb creatures were commanded to be sacrificed as an atonement; therefore their innocent blood was to be shed for the remission of sins: because the Lamb of God, in the fulfilment of His perfect obedience, and the endurance of the great mystery of pain, should, as matter of fact, pour out His blood on the cross a willing sacrifice, an all-sufficing atonement for the sins of the world. It is the idea of the sacrifice of the innocent for the guilty which may be said to underlie and ennoble all the sacrifices of the Law, which sacrifices could not indeed be willing, but only unconscious. This idea is truly divine; and worthily and gloriously was it carried out by the Son of God and Son of man, our beloved Lord and Saviour.

It was then, my brethren, as we may word it, our Lord's voluntary obedience, as the first-born and representative of creation, combined with His voluntary endurance of the anguish of desolation on the cross of Calvary, which amply satisfied the justice and the love of God. And what was this unspeakable anguish? The bodily sufferings of our dear Master, intense as these might be, were but a small part of this anguish. It consisted above all, we may venture to say, in the mental desolation arising from His Father's face being hidden from our Master by the thick cloud of our sins. The more mysterious aspect of our Master's work may never by Christians be ignored. The agony, the desolation, the death, must not be looked on as mere consequences of the obedience. The obedience, broadly speaking, only satisfied justice; it was the voluntary suffering which made appeal to love. God allowed evil, and allowed His creatures to endure it. He then would share the cup of pain. But this opens up another theme again within the recesses of Godhead. In the Atonement obedience and suffering suffice, and both together make our Lord the offering for the sins of the world.

The obedience unto death! Ay, that sufficed to satisfy the Father's justice. At last one creature fulfilled perfectly the will of God from the cradle to the grave; for Christ Jesus accomplished that which Adam and all his race so far had failed to do. Christ stood where all others had fallen without exception, though He was tempted as Adam had been tempted. At length God beheld the true glory of His creation, He beheld *a perfect man*, with liberty to fall or stand. At length the goodness of the Creator was reflected back in the glory of the creature in the man Christ Jesus, the Son of Mary. But had our Lord's obedience not been tried to the very uttermost, we should not have known its exceeding depth, and width, and height: therefore, also, for our instruction was His obedience tried unto the end, that we might be blest in His great example. But as the obedience satisfied Divine Justice, so did the voluntary anguish satisfy the Divine Love. If we stop short of discerning this, our view will be cold and hard. Yea, for Deity, the endurance of suffering in Christ our Lord possessed an infinite value. It appealed to the all-compassionate heart of Deity pure and absolute. Deep called unto deep indeed. And as our dear Lord unfolded one after another those perfections, those boundless abysses of voluntary love and suffering which centre in Him, the heart of Deity was surely turned towards man,

His noblest creation, with an alway waxing intensity of love. The link between God and man which had been broken in Adam and his sinful descendants was as it were riveted anew in Christ our Lord. And as in Adam the human race had fallen, so in Christ did that race rise to stand for evermore. Moreover, reckoning both onward and backward,—onward to the day of final judgment, and backward to the day of man's creation,—the perfections of the Redeemer should be accepted in lieu of the imperfections of the redeemed. God and man were again made at one as before the fall in Christ the Lord. And His "obedience unto death" it was which brought about this full atonement, which "obtained eternal redemption for us."

And one word more before we pass to the close. It becomes us to remember that man's sins were the revealed cause of the incarnate work and marvellous death of Christ our Lord. If man had obeyed his Maker, then it may be that that example of perfect voluntary obedience had not been needed. But as it was He bore our sins, the sins of all mankind, upon the cross. Sin must be punished; and He who was sinned against bore in some mysterious, some most awful and yet most blessed sense the punishment in

His sinful creatures' stead. For "He was wounded for our transgressions, He was bruised for our iniquities."

And now for some few final words respecting our Master's obedience unto death, in its most gracious aspect, as satisfying the love of God. But how can it be fitly spoken of? All our blessed Lord's life leads up to it indeed. But it is as His enemies press upon Him more fiercely that we discern the exceeding, the unspeakable beauty of that obedience, of that atoning work, its patience, its love, its heavenly perfections one and all. It is in the closing scenes of His life and on the cross that Christ Jesus stands revealed to us as "obedient unto death." Oh that His obedience might inspire us in our turn with the urgent, the imperative desire to obey our Heavenly Father's will! Oh that we might also imitate and strive to make our own, by the Holy Spirit's aid, something of the treasures of sweetness, of the manly generosity, and greatness of heart, which lie hidden in our Lord's obedience unto death,—say rather, which are therein manifested to loving eyes and to earnest hearts.

May what has been said to-day, dear brethren, help us to understand in part the great mystery of the Atonement—help us to see in the blood of Jesus Christ a seal and a sign of that obedience unto death by which the Father was pleased to reconcile to Himself a disobedient and fallen world. Therefore let us adore our blessed Redeemer for each several act of His obedience and His love. Let us adore Him for each indignity willingly endured. Let us adore Him most of all when, stricken, reviled, and crucified, He pours forth His precious blood to obtain for us eternal redemption, and calls us to abiding union with His love.

III.
SELF-SURRENDER

SELF-SURRENDER.

St. Mark xiv. 36.

"And He said, Abba, Father, all things are possible unto Thee; take away this cup from Me: nevertheless not what I will, but what Thou wilt."

THE prayer of the text, my dear brethren, thrice repeated, sets before us the mind of the Man Christ Jesus when, in the garden of Gethsemane, on the night before His crucifixion, He turned for help and relief to His Heavenly Father in the hour of utmost weakness and distress. The time long foreseen, the time of a shameful death and of unspeakable spiritual desolation, to be preceded by countless indignities, was at hand: and firmly bent as the Son of Man had ever been to do His Father's will, resolutely as He had ever followed the path of obedience which as He had known all along must lead at last to Calvary, He yet shrank as man with a natural shrinking of flesh and spirit from the dreadful, the tremendous end.

Accordingly, what this oppressed, afflicted Man asked of His Heavenly Father in effect was this :— " Was there not—oh surely might there not be—some other way of manifesting obedience than by continuing to tread the way of uttermost anguish which led to Calvary and to a fearful death ? Was there no other way than *that* by which He, the Friend of sinners, might make atonement for the sins of the world ? Must He indeed die under such appalling circumstances, in such utter desolation, and by such a death ?" It was a heart-rending, a soul-upheaving prayer as in a moral earthquake, so to speak. No like request is recorded as having been addressed of old by the youthful Isaac, our Lord's antetype, to his father Abraham. Isaac did but ask, " My father . . . where is the lamb for a burnt offering ? " And that was doubtless well. For it might have surpassed even Abraham's matchless fortitude to have said " No " to a plea for mercy from the lips of his only son. And, dear brethren, once more to recur to an awful yet most gracious theme full of love and wonder, what it may have cost the Almighty Father's heart to set aside the plea of His Well-beloved, who shall say? since we, with our hard hearts, are deeply moved when we but hear of it. It is when we see our beloved Master as man in His hour of uttermost weakness that He becomes so unspeakably endeared to us; for it is then that we realize most fully the truth of His humanity, of His fellowship with us, the fact that He was and is our Brother and our Friend of friends.

Let us now endeavour to take into our calm consideration the very words of the text. Our Lord had fallen on the ground in prayer. "And He said, Abba, Father, all things are possible unto Thee." How suggestive, how grandly suggestive, are these opening words addressed to the Almighty Father! Who indeed shall shorten the arm of the Lord? These great words, "All things are possible unto Thee," seem to signify no less than this: "If Thou *wilt* Thou canst save the world even without My death upon the cross. If Thou *wilt*, O Father, I may redeem fallen humanity without bearing to the uttermost, at least in such a form, the burden of the sins of the whole world. If Thou *wilt* Thou canst pardon sinners, it may be, without exposing Me, Thy well-beloved, to the utmost malice of the people and the fury of all the powers of darkness. If Thou *wilt*,—" ALL THINGS are possible unto Thee."

And then followed the direct, the wondrous prayer, "Take away this cup from Me." What an appeal, my brethren! See the world's Redeemer in the hour of His uttermost distress. He who said of old through the lips of the prophetic psalmist to the God that delighted not in burnt offerings, "Lo! I come to do Thy will, O God; I am content to do it," He looks up now and asks—ay, it is even so—asks if He may not be spared perchance from extremest intensity of anguish. Is Christ then no longer content, the careless might ask, to do His Father's will? Yea, verily. Not one gracious, not one glorious purpose can be stayed, not one needful sacrifice can be refused. But *must* the path of obedience lead to Calvary? Was ever appeal to pity like unto that, "Take away this cup from Me?" How many a man, brethren, has raised this cry looking up to heaven for some relief, and the relief has followed? And was it not possible, then, we may feel moved to inquire, for the Almighty Father to relent towards His Only-begotten Son, even as it had been possible for Him to stay Abraham's uplifted arm when about to slay his child? Ah, what a spectacle did our Lord present to a gracious Father's eye! Extreme distress, utter agony of mind had driven Him as man to His knees to ask, if it might be, for some lightening of a tremendous, an unspeakable burden, that seemed beyond the endurance of all human powers. And so intense was the agony that His sweat was, as it were, great drops of blood falling down to the ground. "Take away this cup from Me!" Oh, it was indeed a heart-rending cry to us creatures. And if heart-rending for us, brethren, what must it have been then to *the Father?* Whether—we may almost venture to ask in lowly love—was it more dreadful for the Father to afflict or for the Son to be afflicted? Do we feel most for Abraham the father or for Isaac the child upon Mount Moriah? Herein, then, we may faintly, feebly, distantly understand how the whole work of the Atonement is of the Father's love as well as of the Son's boundless self-surrender, and more, I may add, of the Holy Spirit's yearning tenderness: one of the most undoubted truths indeed of the Catholic faith which was in the beginning delivered to the saints. Which of us, my brethren, I ask again, can pass by Abraham in the history of Isaac's sacrifice? Then let us not forget the Almighty Father or the Holy Spirit, and the love and devotion due to the Father and the Spirit, when we contemplate the sacrifice of the Eternal Son. For in the Unity of Godhead and Trinity of Persons is oneness of purpose and of love, unsearchable, supreme; and we must recognize the same infinite love in Father, Son, and Holy Spirit as accomplishing the wondrous work of our redemption.

But the glory of our Blessed Master's prayer, its distinctive glory, that which sets forth His matchless grace of self-surrender, is found most directly in the close. That close runs thus—in the act of self-surrender, disclaiming all desire on our Lord's part to have His own human will fulfilled apart from the will of the Father: " Nevertheless, NOT WHAT I WILL, BUT WHAT THOU WILT." A blessed ending is this to all prayer from man to God; an ending which takes the sting from God's possible denial of our petition, whilst it surely inclines the All-wise to grant with redoubled willingness, if that could be, the thing asked for, so that it be for our true and lasting good. Thus having asked that this cup might pass from Him, our Lord ended by proving, by rendering evident, to men and angels that His will was conformed entirely to the will of His Heavenly Father. Never indeed was the will of the Son of Man at variance with that of His Heavenly Father. His truthful lips had all along proclaimed, " I seek not Mine own will, but the will of the Father which hath sent Me," and again, " For I came down from heaven not to do Mine own will, but the will of Him that sent Me." So then bound up inseparably with our Master's prayer were the great words, "Nevertheless not what I will, but what Thou wilt." And when His Father's will was once fully apprehended, then there could be no wavering, no, not for a single instant. Then did our gracious Master "become obedient unto death, even the death of the cross." He "set His face like a flint." "He hid not His face from shame and spitting." "My punishment is greater than I can bear," guilty Cain had cried of old to the Lord. "Nevertheless not as I will, but as Thou wilt," said the spotless Saviour to the Father.

And verily the Heavenly Father's heart, in the midst of intensest sympathy with His beloved Son, would be satisfied, would be delighted, by this noble self-surrender, by this perfect trust, by this boundless and perfect acquiescence. And that self-surrender was accepted. For although it be most true that all things are possible to God, yet, as we also know, the Father did not see fit to provide any other atonement for the sins of the world than the Lamb *slain* from the foundation of the world. God had provided Himself a Lamb for a burnt offering, even His Only-begotten Son, and though He spared Isaac, yet "He . . . spared not His own Son, but delivered Him up for us all." He loved His Son with a love of which the love of

Abraham for Isaac was but a faint, an inconceivably distant type; and "yet it pleased the Lord to bruise Him." For by His Son's obedience unto death, and by no other means, as we may boldly say, would He save a guilty world; and therefore "the Lord hath laid on Him the iniquity of us all," "and He bare the sin of many."

Now doubtless it was for *our* sakes, brethren, that our dear Master's sufferings were made so exceeding bitter; and the record of them has been made to rouse our sluggish hearts, to kindle them, if that could be, into the flame of love. And each of our Lord's sufferings in turn should endear Him to true Christian hearts the more. Could we bear, we might almost ask in our weakness, to part with one of those wondrous sufferings? Verily, at the least, they are our inheritance of love and pity, and intensest sympathy. For our sakes, yea, and it may be in some deep and hidden sense even for His own sake,—for the sake at the least of everlasting right, for the perfect fulfilment of the Divine will in one creature's perfection, for the obedience of the firstborn of every creature, the representative of wide creation, tried by uttermost suffering even unto death,—for this the Father claimed the sacrifice of "the Lamb" "who verily was foreordained before the foundation of the world:" for by no other means, as far as we can see at least, could God's love for man be made so gloriously apparent, "that our faith and hope might be in God;" and by no other means, we may venture to add, could that creature obedience be tried to the very uttermost and yet prevail.

Now then, dear brethren, we can each one of us say and feel, what amazing proof has not the Father given me of His surpassing love, in suffering His wellbeloved Son to die for me! How boundless was the self-surrender of the Son who died! And how unwearying is the love of the Holy Spirit who has borne and striven with my hard heart so long!

And as on this day the Son of God was lifted up for me a sinner,—how then shall I best please my crucified Lord and Master? how best show forth my love and adoration? For one thing, by trust, by hearty resignation to God's will. In the hour when our Lord prayed, "Take away this cup from Me," how fervently, beloved brethren, should we, if alive and conscious, have joined in that petition for Him! And yet we now see and know that all was ordered for the best. And to-day we do not wish, we cannot wish, our Master's prayer for relief in that hour to have attained its merely human end. So then, beloved brethren, when from our own shrinking lips at any season whatsoever the cup of pain or trial is not removed, despite our prayers,—the cup of sorrow, of disappointment, or of loss,—let us rest assured that only love, yes, only divine and infinite love, holds it there: and let us be content to trust. Let us resolve this very day, by the Holy Spirit's grace, to have, as far as He will help us, no other will than the will of God. Let us surrender ourselves freely and willingly to His good, His blessed providence. Let us lay down our rough, changeful, ofttimes foolish wills at the foot of the Cross. And if even troubles which seem intolerable should ever beset us round about, let us too pray, "Abba, Father, all things are possible unto Thee ; take away this cup from me : NEVERTHELESS, NOT WHAT I WILL, BUT WHAT THOU WILT."

THE END.

GILBERT & RIVINGTON, PRINTERS, ST. JOHN'S SQUARE, LONDON.

NEW BOOKS

IN COURSE OF PUBLICATION BY

MESSRS. RIVINGTON

WATERLOO PLACE, LONDON

HIGH STREET, OXFORD; TRINITY STREET, CAMBRIDGE

July, 1872

THE BOOK OF CHURCH LAW. *Being an Exposition of the Legal Rights and Duties of the Clergy and Laity of the Church of England. By the* Rev. JOHN HENRY BLUNT, M.A., F.S.A. *Revised by* WALTER G. F. PHILLIMORE, B.C.L., *Barrister-at-Law, and Chancellor of the Diocese of Lincoln.*
Crown 8vo. 7s. 6d.

HENRI PERREYVE. *By* A. GRATRY, *Prêtre de l'Oratoire, Professeur de Morale Evangélique à la Sorbonne, et Membre de l'Académie Française. Translated, by special permission, by the Author of* "A Dominican Artist," "Life of S. Francis de Sales," *&c., &c.*
With Portrait. Crown 8vo. 7s. 6d.

NOTITIA EUCHARISTICA. *A Commentary, Explanatory, Doctrinal, and Historical, on the Order of the Administration of the Lord's Supper, or Holy Communion, according to the use of the Church of England. By* W. E. SCUDAMORE, M.A., *Rector of Ditchingham, and formerly Fellow of St. John's College, Cambridge.*
8vo. 28s.

LONDON, OXFORD, AND CAMBRIDGE

B

Messrs. Rivington's

A Selection from the Spiritual Letters of S. Francis de Sales, Bishop and Prince of Geneva.
Translated by the Author of "*Life of S. Francis de Sales,*" "*A Dominican Artist,*" &c., &c.
Crown 8vo. 6s.

Fifteen Sermons preached before the University of Oxford, between A.D. 1826 and 1843.
By John Henry Newman, B.D., *some time Fellow of Oriel College, Oxford.*

Printed uniformly with the "Parochial and Plain Sermons."
New Edition. Crown 8vo. 5s.

The Book of Lessons. *Containing the Proper Psalms and Lessons for Sundays and Holy Days, together with the Daily Lessons from the Calendar, printed in full, according to the New Table of Lessons.*
Crown 8vo. 9s.

Vita et Doctrina Jesu Christi; or, Meditations on the Life of our Lord.
By Avancini. *In the Original Latin. Adapted to the use of the Church of England by a* Clergyman.
Imperial 32mo. 2s. 6d.

The Annotated Book of Common Prayer. *Being an Historical, Ritual, and Theological Commentary on the Devotional System of the Church of England.*
Edited by John Henry Blunt, M.A., F.S.A.
Sixth Edition, Revised. Imperial 8vo. 36s.

WATERLOO PLACE, PALL MALL, LONDON

New Publications.

THE ARGUMENT DELIVERED BEFORE THE JUDICIAL COMMITTEE OF THE PRIVY COUNCIL. *By* ARCHIBALD JOHN STEPHENS, Q.C. *in the case of* THOMAS BYARD SHEPPARD *against* WILLIAM EARLY BENNETT, *Clerk. With an Appendix containing their Lordships' Judgment.*
8vo. 9s.

LATIN PROSE EXERCISES. *Being easy graduated English Sentences for Translation into Latin, with Rules, Explanations, a Vocabulary, and Index. Intended for the Use of Beginners and Junior Forms of Schools. By* R. PROWDE SMITH, B.A., *Assistant Master at the Grammar School, Henley-on-Thames.*
Crown 8vo. 2s. 6d.

LECTURES ON THE RE-UNION OF THE CHRISTIAN CHURCHES. *By* JOHN J. IGN. VON DÖLLINGER. Revised by the Author after delivery. Authorised Translation.
Crown 8vo. [*In the Press.*

THE LAST DAYS OF PÈRE GRATRY. *By* PÈRE ADOLPHE PERRAUD, *of the Oratory, and Professor of La Sorbonne. Translated by special permission.*
Crown 8vo. 3s. 6d.

THE KNIGHT OF INTERCESSION, AND OTHER POEMS. *By the* REV. S. J. STONE, M.A., *Pembroke College, Oxford, Author of "The Thanksgiving Hymn on the Recovery of the Prince of Wales."*
Small 8vo.

AND AT OXFORD, AND CAMBRIDGE

Messrs. Rivington's

EIGHT LECTURES ON THE MIRACLES.
Being the Bampton Lectures for 1865. By J. B. MOZLEY, D.D., *Regius Professor of Divinity, and Canon of Christ Church, Oxford.*

Third Edition, Revised. Crown 8vo. 7s. 6d.

WORDS TO TAKE WITH US. *A Manual of Daily and Occasional Prayers, for Private and Common Use. With plain Instructions and Counsels on Prayer.* By W. E. SCUDAMORE, M.A., *Rector of Ditchingham, and formerly Fellow of St. John's College, Cambridge.*

New Edition, Revised. Small 8vo. 2s. 6d.

A SHADOW OF DANTE. *Being an Essay towards studying Himself, his World, and his Pilgrimage.* By MARIA FRANCESCA ROSSETTI.

With Illustrations. Crown 8vo. 10s. 6d.

A THEORY OF HARMONY. *Founded on the Tempered Scale. With Questions and Exercises for the use of Students.* By JOHN STAINER, MUS. DOC., M.A., *Magd. Coll., Oxon, Organist to St. Paul's Cathedral.*

Second Edition. 8vo. 7s. 6d.

SELECTIONS FROM LUCIAN. *With English Notes.* By EVELYN ABBOTT, *Assistant Master in Clifton College.*

Small 8vo. [*In the Press.*

WATERLOO PLACE, PALL MALL, LONDON

New Publications.

The Holy Catholic Church: its
Divine Ideal, Ministry, and Institutions. *A Short Treatise. With a Catechism on each Chapter, forming a Course of Methodical Instruction on the subject.* By Edward Meyrick Goulburn, D.D., *Dean of Norwich.*
Crown 8vo. [In the Press.

A Handy Book on the Ecclesias-
tical Dilapidations Act, 1871. *With Remarks on the Qualification and Practice of Diocesan Surveyors.* By Edward G. Bruton, *Fellow of the Royal Institute of British Architects, and Diocesan Surveyor, Oxford.*
Crown 8vo. 3s. 6d.

Sermons on Certain of the Less
Prominent Facts and References in Sacred Story. By Henry Melvill, B.D., *late Canon of St. Paul's, and Chaplain in Ordinary to the Queen.*
New Edition. Two vols. Crown 8vo. 5s. each.

Some Elements of Religion. Lent
Lectures. By Henry Parry Liddon, D.D., D.C.L., *Canon of St. Paul's, and Ireland Professor of Exegesis in the University of Oxford.*
Crown 8vo. 5s.

Aids to Prayer; or, Thoughts on
the Practice of Devotion. *With Forms of Prayer for Private Use.* By Daniel Moore, M.A., *Chaplain in Ordinary to the Queen, and Vicar of Holy Trinity, Paddington, Author of "Sermons on Special Occasions."*
Second Edition. Square 32mo. 2s. 6d.

AND AT OXFORD, AND CAMBRIDGE

Messrs. Rivington's

Scenes from Greek Plays. *Rugby Edition.*
Abridged and adapted for the use of Schools, by ARTHUR SIDGWICK, M.A., *Assistant Master at Rugby School, and formerly Fellow of Trinity College, Cambridge.*

ARISTOPHANES. *The Clouds. The Frogs. The Knights. Plutus.*

EURIPIDES. *Iphigenia in Tauris. The Cyclops.*

Small 8vo. 1s. 6d. each, or 1s. in paper cover.

Church Organs: *Their Position and Construction.*
With an Appendix containing some Account of the Mediæval Organ Case still existing at Old Radnor, South Wales. By FREDERICK HEATHCOTE SUTTON, M.A., *Vicar of Theddingworth.*

With Illustrations. Imperial folio. 6s. 6d.

The Path of Holiness: *A First Book*
of Prayers, with the Service of the Holy Communion, for the Young. Compiled by a Priest. Edited by the Rev. T. T. CARTER, M.A., *Rector of Clewer, Berks.*

With Illustrations. Crown 16mo, 1s. 6d., or limp cloth, 1s.

Progressive Exercises in Latin Elegiac Verse.
By C. G. GEPP, B.A., *late Junior Student of Christ Church, Oxford, and Assistant Master at Tonbridge School.*

Second Edition, Revised. Crown 8vo. 3s. 6d.

WATERLOO PLACE, PALL MALL, LONDON

New Publications.

THE ATHANASIAN ORIGIN OF THE ATHANASIAN CREED. By J. S. BREWER, M.A., Preacher at the Rolls, and Honorary Fellow of Queen's College, Oxford.

Crown 8vo. 3s. 6d.

THE THIRTY-NINE ARTICLES OF THE CHURCH OF ENGLAND EXPLAINED IN A SERIES OF LECTURES. By the REV. R. W. JELF, D.D., late Canon of Christ Church, Oxford, and sometime Principal of King's College, London. Edited by the REV. J. R. KING, M.A., Vicar of St. Peter's in the East, Oxford, and formerly Fellow and Tutor of Merton College.

8vo. [In the Press.

S. FRANCIS DE SALES, BISHOP AND PRINCE OF GENEVA. By the Author of "A Dominican Artist," "Life of Madame Louise de France," &c., &c.

New Edition. Crown 8vo. 6s.

HISTORICAL NARRATIVES. From the Russian. By H. C. ROMANOFF, Author of "Sketches of the Rites and Customs of the Greco-Russian Church," &c.

Crown 8vo. 6s.

THE WAY OF LIFE. A Book of Prayers and Instruction for the Young at School. Compiled by a Priest. Edited by the REV. T. T. CARTER, M.A., Rector of Clewer, Berks.

Imperial 32mo. 1s. 6d.

AND AT OXFORD, AND CAMBRIDGE

Messrs. Rivington's

THOUGHTS ON PERSONAL RELIGION.

Being a Treatise on the Christian Life in its Two Chief Elements, Devotion and Practice. By EDWARD MEYRICK GOULBURN, D.D., *Dean of Norwich.*

New Presentation Edition, elegantly printed on Toned Paper. Two vols. Small 8vo. 10s. 6d.

An Edition in one vol., 6s. 6d.; also, a CHEAP EDITION, 3s. 6d.

A CHURCH HISTORY OF THE FIRST SEVEN CENTURIES, TO THE CLOSE OF THE SIXTH GENERAL COUNCIL.

By MILO MAHAN, D.D., *sometime S. Mark's-in-the-Bowery Professor of Ecclesiastical History in the General Theological Seminary, New York.*

8vo. 15s.

ENGLISH NURSERY RHYMES. TRANSLATED INTO FRENCH.

By JOHN ROBERTS, M.A., *Fellow of Magdalene College, Cambridge.*

Square 16mo. 2s. 6d.

THE SPIRIT OF S. FRANCIS DE SALES,

Bishop and Prince of Geneva. Translated from the French by the Author of "*The Life of S. Francis de Sales,*" "*A Dominican Artist,*" &c., &c.

Crown 8vo. 6s.

OUR MOTHER CHURCH. *Being Simple Talk on High Topics.* By ANNE MERCIER.

Crown 8vo. [*Nearly Ready.*

WATERLOO PLACE, PALL MALL, LONDON

New Publications.

DICTIONARY OF DOCTRINAL AND HISTORICAL THEOLOGY. *By Various Writers. Edited by the* REV. JOHN HENRY BLUNT, M.A., F.S.A., *Editor of "The Annotated Book of Common Prayer."*

Second Edition. Imperial 8vo. 42s.

THE PSALMS. *Translated from the Hebrew.*
With Notes, chiefly Exegetical. By WILLIAM KAY, D.D., *Rector of Great Leighs; late Principal of Bishop's College, Calcutta.*

8vo. 12s. 6d.

SERMONS. *By* HENRY MELVILL, B.D., *late Canon of St. Paul's, and Chaplain in Ordinary to the Queen.*

New Edition. Two vols. Crown 8vo. 5s. each.

THE ORIGIN AND DEVELOPMENT OF RELIGIOUS BELIEF. *By* S. BARING-GOULD, M.A., *Author of "Curious Myths of the Middle Ages."*

Vol. I. Monotheism and Polytheism. Second Edition. 8vo. 15s.
Vol. II. Christianity. 8vo. 15s.

PARISH MUSINGS; OR, DEVOTIONAL POEMS. *By* JOHN S. B. MONSELL, LL.D., *Rural Dean, and Rector of St. Nicholas, Guildford.*

Fine Edition. Small 8vo. 5s.
Cheap Edition, 18mo, limp cloth, 1s. 6d.; or in cover, 1s.

AND AT OXFORD, AND CAMBRIDGE

Messrs. Rivington's

SERMONS ON SPECIAL OCCASIONS. By
DANIEL MOORE, M.A., *Chaplain in Ordinary to the Queen, and Vicar of Holy Trinity, Paddington; Author of "Aids to Prayer," &c.*

Crown 8vo. 7s. 6d.

PRAYERS AND MEDITATIONS FOR THE
HOLY COMMUNION. *With a Preface by* C. J. ELLICOTT, D.D., *Lord Bishop of Gloucester and Bristol.*

With Rubrics in red. Royal 32mo. 2s. 6d.

MATERIALS AND MODELS FOR GREEK
AND LATIN PROSE COMPOSITION. *Selected and arranged by* J. Y. SARGENT, M.A., *Tutor, late Fellow of Magdalen College, Oxford;* and T. F. DALLIN, M.A., *Fellow and Tutor of Queen's College, Oxford.*

Crown 8vo. 7s. 6d.

THE STAR OF CHILDHOOD. *A First Book of Prayers and Instruction for Children. Compiled by a Priest. Edited by the* REV. T. T. CARTER, M.A., *Rector of Clewer, Berks.*

With Illustrations, reduced from Engravings by FRA ANGELICO.
Royal 16mo. 2s. 6d.

SELF-RENUNCIATION. *From the French.*
With Introduction by the REV. T. T. CARTER, M.A., *Rector of Clewer, Berks.*

Crown 8vo. 6s.

WATERLOO PLACE, PALL MALL, LONDON

New Publications.

THE HIDDEN LIFE OF THE SOUL.

From the French. By the Author of "*A Dominican Artist*," "*Life of Madame Louise de France*," &c., &c.

Crown 8vo. 5s.

ANCIENT HYMNS. *From the Roman Breviary.*

For Domestic Use every Morning and Evening of the Week, and on the Holy Days of the Church. To which are added, Original Hymns, principally of Commemoration and Thanksgiving for Christ's Holy Ordinances. By RICHARD MANT, D.D., sometime Lord Bishop of Down and Connor.

New Edition. Small 8vo. 5s.

THE TWO BROTHERS, *and other Poems.*

By EDWARD HENRY BICKERSTETH, M.A., Vicar of Christ Church, Hampstead, and Chaplain to the Bishop of Ripon, Author of "*Yesterday, To-day, and for Ever.*"

Second Edition. Small 8vo. 6s.

ST. JOHN CHRYSOSTOM'S LITURGY.

Translated by H. C. ROMANOFF, Author of "*Sketches of the Rites and Customs of the Greco-Russian Church.*"

With Illustrations. Square crown 8vo. 4s. 6d.

THE LIFE OF JUSTIFICATION. *A Series*

of Lectures delivered in Substance at All Saints', Margaret Street, in Lent, 1870. By the REV. GEORGE BODY, B.A., Rector of Kirkby Misperton.

Second Edition. Crown 8vo. 4s. 6d.

AND AT OXFORD, AND CAMBRIDGE

Messrs. Rivington's

The "Damnatory Clauses" of the Athanasian Creed rationally Explained, in a Letter to the Right Hon. W. E. Gladstone, M.P. *By the* Rev. Malcolm MacColl, M.A., *Rector of St. George, Botolph Lane.*

Crown 8vo. 6s.

The Sayings of the Great Forty Days, *between the Resurrection and Ascension, regarded as the Outlines of the Kingdom of God. In Five Discourses. With an Examination of Dr. Newman's Theory of Development. By* George Moberly, D.C.L., *Bishop of Salisbury.*

Fourth Edition. Crown 8vo. 7s. 6d.

A Plain Account of the English Bible. *From the Earliest Times of its Translation to the Present Day. By* John Henry Blunt, M.A., *Vicar of Kennington, Oxford; Editor of "The Annotated Book of Common Prayer," &c.*

Crown 8vo. 3s. 6d.

The Pope and the Council. *By* Janus. *Authorised Translation from the German.*

Third Edition, Revised. Crown 8vo. 7s. 6d.

Letters from Rome on the Council. *By* Quirinus. *Reprinted from the "*Allgemeine Zeitung.*" Authorised Translation.*

Crown 8vo. 12s.

WATERLOO PLACE, PALL MALL, LONDON

New Publications.

DIRECTORIUM PASTORALE. *The Principles and Practice of Pastoral Work in the Church of England.* By the REV. JOHN HENRY BLUNT, M.A., F.S.A., *Editor of "The Annotated Book of Common Prayer," &c., &c.*

Third Edition, Revised. Crown 8vo. 7s. 6d.

THE FIRST BOOK OF COMMON PRAYER OF EDWARD VI. AND THE ORDINAL OF 1549. *Together with the Order of the Communion,* 1548. *Reprinted entire, and Edited by the* REV. HENRY BASKERVILLE WALTON, M.A., *late Fellow and Tutor of Merton College; with Introduction by the* REV. PETER GOLDSMITH MEDD, M.A., *Senior Fellow and Tutor of University College, Oxford.*

Small 8vo. 6s.

THE PURSUIT OF HOLINESS. *A Sequel to "Thoughts on Personal Religion," intended to carry the Reader somewhat farther onward in the Spiritual Life.* By EDWARD MEYRICK GOULBURN, D.D., *Dean of Norwich.*

Fourth Edition. Small 8vo. 5s.

APOSTOLICAL SUCCESSION IN THE CHURCH OF ENGLAND. *By the* REV. ARTHUR W. HADDAN, B.D., *Rector of Barton-on-the-Heath, and late Fellow of Trinity College, Oxford.*

8vo. 12s.

AND AT OXFORD, AND CAMBRIDGE

Messrs. Rivington's

THE PRIEST TO THE ALTAR; or, Aids to the Devout Celebration of Holy Communion; chiefly after the Ancient Use of Sarum.

Second Edition. Enlarged, Revised, and Re-arranged with the Secretæ, Post-communion, &c., appended to the Collects, Epistles, and Gospels, throughout the Year.

8vo. 7s. 6d.

PAROCHIAL AND PLAIN SERMONS. By JOHN HENRY NEWMAN, B.D., *formerly Vicar of St. Mary's, Oxford. Edited by the* REV. W. J. COPELAND, *Rector of Farnham, Essex.*

From the Text of the last Editions published by MESSRS. RIVINGTON.

New Edition. Eight vols. Crown 8vo. 5s. each.

SERMONS BEARING ON SUBJECTS OF THE DAY. *By* JOHN HENRY NEWMAN, B.D. *Edited by the* REV. W. J. COPELAND, *Rector of Farnham, Essex.*

With Index of Dates of all the Sermons.

New Edition. Crown 8vo. 5s.

BRIGHSTONE SERMONS. *By* GEORGE MOBERLY, D.C.L., *Bishop of Salisbury.*

Second Edition. Crown 8vo. 7s. 6d.

WATERLOO PLACE, PALL MALL, LONDON

New Publications.

THE CHARACTERS OF THE OLD TESTAMENT. *A Series of Sermons.* By the REV. ISAAC WILLIAMS, B.D., *late Fellow of Trinity College, Oxford.*

New Edition. Crown 8vo. 5s.

FEMALE CHARACTERS OF HOLY SCRIPTURE. *A Series of Sermons.* By the REV. ISAAC WILLIAMS, B.D., *late Fellow of Trinity College, Oxford.*

New Edition. Crown 8vo. 5s.

THE DIVINITY OF OUR LORD AND SAVIOUR JESUS CHRIST. *Being the Bampton Lectures for 1866.* By HENRY PARRY LIDDON, D.D., D.C.L., *Canon of St. Paul's, and Ireland Professor of Exegesis in the University of Oxford.*

Fifth Edition. Crown 8vo. 5s.

SERMONS PREACHED BEFORE THE UNIVERSITY OF OXFORD. By HENRY PARRY LIDDON, D.D., D.C.L., *Canon of St. Paul's, and Ireland Professor of Exegesis in the University of Oxford.*

Fourth Edition. Crown 8vo. 5s.

A MANUAL FOR THE SICK. *With other Devotions.* By LAUNCELOT ANDREWES, D.D., *sometime Lord Bishop of Winchester. Edited, with a Preface,* by HENRY PARRY LIDDON, D.D., D.C.L., *Canon of St. Paul's.*

With Portrait. Second Edition. Large type. 24mo. 2s. 6d.

AND AT OXFORD, AND CAMBRIDGE

Messrs. Rivington's

WALTER KERR HAMILTON, BISHOP OF SALISBURY. *A Sketch.* By HENRY PARRY LIDDON, D.D., D.C.L., *Canon of St. Paul's.*

Second Edition. 8vo. 2s. 6d.
Or, bound with the Sermon "Life in Death," 3s. 6d.

THE LIFE OF MADAME LOUISE DE FRANCE, *Daughter of Louis XV., known also as the Mother Térèse de S. Augustin. By the Author of* "*A Dominican Artist,*" *&c.* Crown 8vo. 6s.

INSTRUCTIONS FOR THE USE OF CANDIDATES FOR HOLY ORDERS, AND OF THE PAROCHIAL CLERGY; *with Acts of Parliament relating to the same, and Forms proposed to be used.* By CHRISTOPHER HODGSON, M.A., *Secretary to the Governors of Queen Anne's Bounty.*

Ninth Edition, Revised and Enlarged. 8vo. 16s.

THE TREASURY OF DEVOTION. *A Manual of Prayers for General and Daily Use. Compiled by a Priest. Edited by the* REV. T. T. CARTER, M.A., *Rector of Clewer, Berks.*

Fourth Edition. 16mo, 2s. 6d.; Limp cloth, 2s.
Bound with the Book of Common Prayer, 3s. 6d.

A DOMINICAN ARTIST. *A Sketch of the Life of the Rev. Père Besson, of the Order of St. Dominic. By the Author of* "*The Life of Madame Louise de France,*" *&c.*

Second Edition. Crown 8vo. 6s.

WATERLOO PLACE, PALL MALL, LONDON

New Publications.

THE GUIDE TO HEAVEN. *A Book of Prayers for every Want. (For the Working Classes.) Compiled by a Priest.* Edited by the REV. T. T. CARTER, M.A., *Rector of Clewer, Berks.*
Second Edition. Crown 8vo, 1s. 6d.; Limp cloth, 1s.

THE REFORMATION OF THE CHURCH OF ENGLAND. *Its History, Principles, and Results.* A.D. 1514–1547. By JOHN HENRY BLUNT, M.A., *Vicar of Kennington, Oxford, Editor of "The Annotated Book of Common Prayer," Author of "Directorium Pastorale," &c., &c.*
Second Edition. 8vo. 16s.

THE VIRGIN'S LAMP. *Prayers and Devout Exercises for English Sisters. Chiefly composed and selected by the late* REV. J. M. NEALE, D.D., *Founder of St. Margaret's, East Grinsted.*
Small 8vo. 3s. 6d.

CATECHETICAL NOTES AND CLASS QUESTIONS, LITERAL AND MYSTICAL. *Chiefly on the Earlier Books of Holy Scripture.* By the late REV. J. M. NEALE, D.D., *Warden of Sackville College, East Grinsted.*
Crown 8vo. 5s.

SERMONS FOR CHILDREN. *Being Thirty-three Short Readings, addressed to the Children of St. Margaret's Home, East Grinsted.* By the late REV. J. M. NEALE, D.D., *Warden of Sackville College, East Grinsted.*
Second Edition. Small 8vo. 3s. 6d.

AND AT OXFORD, AND CAMBRIDGE

Messrs. Rivington's

A History of the Holy Eastern
Church. *The Patriarchate of Antioch, to the Middle of the Fifth Century.* By the Rev. John Mason Neale, D.D., *late Warden of Sackville College, East Grinsted. Followed by a History of the Patriarchs of Antioch, translated from the Greek of Constantius I., Patriarch of Constantinople. Edited, with an Introduction, by* George Williams, B.D., *Vicar of Ringwood, late Fellow of King's College, Cambridge.*

8vo. [*In the Press.*

Fables respecting the Popes of
the Middle Ages. *A Contribution to Ecclesiastical History.* By John J. Ign. Von Döllinger. *Translated, with Introduction and Appendices, by* Alfred Plummer, M.A., *Fellow and Tutor of Trinity College, Oxford.*

8vo. 14s.

Physical Facts and Scriptural
Record; or, Eighteen Propositions for Geologists. By W. B. Galloway, M.A., *Vicar of St. Mark's. Regent's Park, and Chaplain to the Right Hon. Lord Viscount Hawarden.*

8vo. 10s. 6d.

Dean Alford's Greek Testament.
With English Notes, intended for the Upper Forms of Schools, and for Pass-men at the Universities. Abridged by Bradley H. Alford, M.A., *late Scholar of Trinity College, Cambridge.*

Crown 8vo. 10s. 6d.

WATERLOO PLACE, PALL MALL, LONDON

New Publications.

HONORÉ DE BALZAC. *Edited, with English Notes and Introductory Notice, by* HENRI VAN LAUN, *formerly French Master at Cheltenham College, and now Master of the French Language and Literature at the Edinburgh Academy.* (*Being the First Volume of "Selections from Modern French Authors."*)

Crown 8vo. 3s. 6d.

H. A. TAINE. *Edited, with English Notes and Introductory Notice, by* HENRI VAN LAUN. (*Being the Second Volume of "Selections from Modern French Authors."*)

Crown 8vo. 3s. 6d.

ARITHMETIC, THEORETICAL AND PRACTICAL. *By* W. H. GIRDLESTONE, M.A., *of Christ's College, Cambridge, Principal of the Theological College, Gloucester.*

New Edition. Crown 8vo. 6s. 6d.
Also an Edition for Schools. Small 8vo. 3s. 6d.

DICTIONARY OF SECTS, HERESIES, AND SCHOOLS OF THOUGHT. *By Various Writers. Edited by the* REV. JOHN HENRY BLUNT, M.A., F.S.A., *Editor of the "Dictionary of Doctrinal and Historical Theology."*

(*Forming the Second Portion of the "Summary of Theology and Ecclesiastical History," which Messrs. Rivington have in course of preparation as a "Thesaurus Theologicus" for the Clergy and Laity of the Church of England.*)

Imperial 8vo. [*In the Press.*

AND AT OXFORD, AND CAMBRIDGE

Messrs. Rivington's

THE APOSTOLIC FATHERS. *The Epistles of S. Clement, S. Ignatius, S. Barnabas, S. Polycarp, together with the Martyrdom of S. Ignatius and S. Polycarp. Translated into English, with an Introductory Notice,* by CHARLES H. HOOLE, M.A., *Senior Student of Christ Church, Oxford.*
Small 8vo. 5s. 6d.

HELP AND COMFORT FOR THE SICK POOR. *By the Author of "Sickness; its Trials and Blessings."*
New Edition. Small 8vo. 1s.

HERODOTI HISTORIA. *Edited by* H. G. WOODS, M.A., *Fellow and Tutor of Trinity College, Oxford.*
Crown 8vo.
Forming a New Part of the "Catena Classicorum."
[*In the Press.*

SKETCHES OF THE RITES AND CUSTOMS OF THE GRECO-RUSSIAN CHURCH. *By* H. C. ROMANOFF. *With an Introductory Notice by the Author of "The Heir of Redclyffe."*
Second Edition. Crown 8vo. 7s. 6d.

HOUSEHOLD THEOLOGY. *A Handbook of Religious Information respecting the Holy Bible, the Prayer Book, the Church, the Ministry, Divine Worship, the Creeds, &c., &c.* By JOHN HENRY BLUNT, M.A.
New Edition. Small 8vo. 3s. 6d.

WATERLOO PLACE, PALL MALL, LONDON

New Publications.

CURIOUS MYTHS OF THE MIDDLE AGES.
By S. BARING-GOULD, M.A., *Author of "Post-Mediæval Preachers," &c.*

With Illustrations. New Edition. Crown 8vo. 6s.

THE PRAYER BOOK INTERLEAVED.
With Historical Illustrations and Explanatory Notes, arranged parallel to the Text. By the REV. W. M. CAMPION, D.D., *Fellow and Tutor of Queen's College, and Rector of St. Botolph's,* and the REV. W. J. BEAMONT, M.A., *late Fellow of Trinity College, Cambridge. With a Preface by the* LORD BISHOP OF ELY.

Sixth Edition. Small 8vo. 7s. 6d.

SICKNESS; ITS TRIALS AND BLESSINGS.
New Edition. Small 8vo. 3s. 6d.
Also a Cheap Edition, 1s. 6d.; or in paper cover, 1s.

HYMNS AND POEMS FOR THE SICK AND SUFFERING.
In connection with the Service for the Visitation of the Sick. Selected from Various Authors. Edited by T. V. FOSBERY, M.A., *Vicar of St. Giles's, Reading.*

New Edition. Small 8vo. 3s. 6d.

MISCELLANEOUS POEMS.
By HENRY FRANCIS LYTE, M.A.

New Edition. Small 8vo. 5s.

AND AT OXFORD, AND CAMBRIDGE

Messrs. Rivington's

The Happiness of the Blessed.

Considered as to the Particulars of their State; their Recognition of each other in that State; and its Differences of Degrees. To which are added, Musings on the Church and her Services. By Richard Mant, D.D., *sometime Lord Bishop of Down and Connor.*

New Edition. Small 8vo. 3s. 6d.

Catechesis; or, Christian Instruction Preparatory to Confirmation and First Communion. By Charles Wordsworth, D.C.L., *Bishop of St. Andrew's.*

New Edition. Small 8vo. 2s.

Warnings of the Holy Week, &c.

Being a Course of Parochial Lectures for the Week before Easter and the Easter Festivals. By the Rev. W. Adams, M.A., *late Vicar of St. Peter's-in-the-East, Oxford, and Fellow of Merton College.*

Seventh Edition. Small 8vo. 4s. 6d.

Consolatio; or, Comfort for the Afflicted. *Edited by the* Rev. C. E. Kennaway. *With a Preface by* Samuel Wilberforce, D.D., *Lord Bishop of Winchester.*

New Edition. Small 8vo. 3s. 6d.

Recollections of Ober-Ammergau in 1871. By Henry Nutcombe Oxenham, M.A., *late Scholar of Balliol College, Oxford.*

Crown 8vo. 3s. 6d.

WATERLOO PLACE, PALL MALL, LONDON

New Publications.

FAMILY PRAYERS. *Compiled from Various Sources (chiefly from Bishop Hamilton's Manual), and arranged on the Liturgical Principle.* By EDWARD MEYRICK GOULBURN, D.D., *Dean of Norwich.*

New Edition. Large type. Crown 8vo, 3s. 6d.
Cheap Edition. 16mo. 1s.

THE ANNUAL REGISTER. *A Review of Public Events at Home and Abroad, for the Year* 1871.
8vo. 18s.

The Volumes of the New Series, 1863 to 1870, may be had, 18s. each.

THE HOME LIFE OF JESUS OF NAZARETH, &c. *By the* REV. AUGUSTUS GURNEY, M.A., *Vicar of Wribbenhall, Kidderminster, in the Diocese of Worcester.*
Crown 8vo. 5s.

A MEMORIAL VOLUME OF SERMONS. *By the late* REV. JOHN HENRY HOLFORD, M.A. *With a Short Biographical Preface.* By the REV. E. H. BICKERSTETH, M.A.
Small 8vo. 5s.

THE GOSPEL OF THE CHILDHOOD. *A Practical and Devotional Commentary on the Single Incident of our Blessed* LORD'S *Childhood (St. Luke* ii. 41, *to the end); designed as a Help to Meditation on the Holy Scriptures, for Children and Young Persons.* By EDWARD MEYRICK GOULBURN, D.D., *Dean of Norwich.*
Square 16mo. [*In the Press.*

AND AT OXFORD, AND CAMBRIDGE

Messrs. Rivington's

Yesterday, To-Day, and For Ever.

A Poem in Twelve Books. By EDWARD HENRY BICKERSTETH, M.A., *Vicar of Christ Church, Hampstead, and Chaplain to the Bishop of Ripon.*

Seventh Edition. Small 8vo. 6s.

A Companion to the Old Testament.

Being a Plain Commentary on Scripture History, down to the Birth of our Lord.

Small 8vo. 3s. 6d.

Sacred Allegories.

The Shadow of the Cross—The Distant Hills—The Old Man's Home—The King's Messengers. By the REV. W. ADAMS, M.A., *late Fellow of Merton College, Oxford.*

With Engravings from Original Designs by Charles W. Cope, R.A., John C. Horsley, A.R.A., Samuel Palmer, Birket Foster, and George Hicks.

The Four Allegories, separately. Crown 8vo. 2s. 6d. each.

A Glossary of Ecclesiastical Terms.

Containing Brief Explanations of Words used in Theology, Liturgiology, Chronology, Law, Architecture, Antiquities, Symbolism, Greek Hierology and Mediæval Latin; together with some account of Titles of our Lord, Emblems of Saints, Hymns, Orders, Heresies, Ornaments, Offices, Vestments and Ceremonial, and Miscellaneous Subjects. By Various Writers. Edited by the REV. ORBY SHIPLEY, M.A.

Crown 8vo. 18s.

WATERLOO PLACE, PALL MALL, LONDON

New Publications.

STONES OF THE TEMPLE; OR, LESSONS FROM THE FABRIC AND FURNITURE OF THE CHURCH.
By WALTER FIELD, M.A., F.S.A., *Vicar of Godmersham.*

With numerous Illustrations. Crown 8vo. 7s. 6d.

LIBER PRECUM PUBLICARUM ECCLESIÆ ANGLICANÆ.
A GULIELMO BRIGHT, A.M., *et* PETRO GOLDSMITH MEDD, A.M., *Presbyteris, Collegii Universitatis in Acad. Oxon. Sociis, Latine redditus.*

New Edition, with all the Rubrics in red. Small 8vo. 6s.

BIBLE READINGS FOR FAMILY PRAYER.
By the REV. W. H. RIDLEY, M.A., *Rector of Hambleden.*

Crown 8vo.

Old Testament—Genesis and Exodus. 2s.

New Testament, 3s. 6d. } St. Matthew and St. Mark. 2s.
St. Luke and St. John. 2s.

SELECT PLAYS OF SHAKSPERE. *Rugby Edition.*
"As You Like It." *Edited by* CHAS. E. MOBERLY, M.A., *Assistant Master in Rugby School.*

Small 8vo. 2s.; or in paper cover, 1s. 6d.

*** *Other Plays are in Preparation.*

AND AT OXFORD, AND CAMBRIDGE

Messrs. Rivington's
New Pamphlets.

CLERGY DISCIPLINE: *A Letter to His Grace the* ARCHBISHOP OF CANTERBURY. *From the Right Hon.* SIR ROBERT PHILLIMORE, *Judge of the Arches Court.*

8vo. 6*d*.

ENGLISH CHURCH DEFENCE TRACTS.

No. 1. ROMAN MISQUOTATIONS.

No. 2. ARE CLERGYMEN OF THE ENGLISH CHURCH RIGHTLY ORDAINED?

No. 3. PAPAL INFALLIBILITY.

No. 4. MORE ABOUT "ROMAN MISQUOTATIONS": IN REPLY TO A PAMPHLET ENTITLED "ANGLICAN MISREPRESENTATIONS."

8vo. 3*d*. each.

REMARKS ON THE MEMORIAL AND PETITION TO CONVOCATION OF THE COUNCIL OF THE ENGLISH CHURCH UNION, *headed respectively "Proposed Legislation on the Prayer-Book" (Jan. 30, 1872), and "Proposed Rubric against Non-Communicating Attendance during the Holy Communion" (April 15, 1872.) By* W. E. SCUDAMORE, *Rector of Ditchingham, Norfolk.*

8vo. 1*s*.

THE PROPOSED CONTROL OF THE PUBLIC SCHOOLS BY THE UNIVERSITIES. *By* EDWARD E. BOWEN, M.A., *Master of the Modern Side, Harrow School.*

8vo. 1*s*.

WATERLOO PLACE, PALL MALL, LONDON

New Publications.

New Pamphlets
ON THE ATHANASIAN CREED.

REPORT OF THE COMMITTEE OF BISHOPS ON THE REVISION OF THE TEXT AND TRANSLATION OF THE ATHANASIAN CREED, *with an Introduction and Notes.* By CHARLES JOHN, Lord Bishop of Gloucester and Bristol. 8vo. 1s.

ON THE ATHANASIAN CREED. *A Speech by the* BISHOP OF LINCOLN *in the Upper House of Convocation, Feb. 8, 1872.* Small 8vo. 1d.

THE TOWERS OF ZION. *A Sermon on the Athanasian Creed, preached in St. Michael and All Angels' Church, Weyhill, on Trinity Sunday, 1871.* By W. H. SIMCOX, M.A., *Rector of Weyhill, late Fellow of Queen's College, Oxford.* 8vo. 6d.

SHOW THE LIGHT AND BLOW THE TRUMPET; *or, Gideon's Good Advice for Dispersing the Midianites applied to the Defence of the Athanasian Creed. A Sermon at St. Cyprian's, on Refreshment Sunday, March 10, 1872, by the* Rev. CHARLES GUTCH, B.D. 8vo. 1s.

THE ATHANASIAN CREED NEITHER UNCHARITABLE NOR TOO ABSTRUSE FOR GENERAL USE. *A Sermon Preached in the Church of the Holy Trinity, Stratford-upon-Avon, on Trinity Sunday, 1872.* By the Rev. RICHARD SEYMOUR, *Rector of Kinwarton, Honorary Canon of Worcester Cathedral, and Proctor for the Clergy of the Diocese.* Crown 8vo. 4d.

THE ATHANASIAN CREED. *With special reference to the so-called Damnatory Clauses and the Proposed Revision of the Translation. A Paper read at a Ruridecanal Chapter. With an Appendix containing an Examination of some Points advanced by Professor Swainson respecting the Creed.* By G. D. W. OMMANNEY, M.A., *Curate of Whitchurch, Somerset.* 8vo. 1s.

IS IT GOD'S TRUTH? IS IT WIDELY RECEIVED AND BELIEVED BY GOD'S CHURCH? *Reasons for neither mutilating nor muffling* THE ATHANASIAN CREED, *but retaining it intact in the Services of the Church.* By EDWARD MEYRICK GOULBURN, D.D., *Dean of Norwich.* 8vo. 1s.

THE ADMONITORY CLAUSES IN THE CHURCH'S HOMILETICAL CREED. *A Letter to the Rev. C. J. Vaughan, D.D., Master of the Temple.* By PHILIP FREEMAN, M.A., *Archdeacon of Exeter.* 8vo. 6d.

WHY A NOTE TO THE ATHANASIAN CREED? *A Letter suggested by that on the Admonitory Clauses of the Church's Homiletical Creed. Addressed, by permission, to the Ven. the Archdeacon of Exeter.* By JOHN PUCKLE, M.A., *Vicar of St. Mary's, Dover, Rural Dean, Proctor in Convocation for the Diocese of Canterbury.* 8vo. 1s.

AND AT OXFORD, AND CAMBRIDGE

Messrs. Rivington's

Keys to Christian Knowledge.

Small 8vo.   2s. 6d. each.

A KEY TO THE KNOWLEDGE AND USE OF THE BOOK OF COMMON PRAYER. *By* JOHN HENRY BLUNT, M.A., *Editor of "The Annotated Book of Common Prayer."*

A KEY TO THE KNOWLEDGE AND USE OF THE HOLY BIBLE. *By* JOHN HENRY BLUNT, M.A.

A KEY TO THE KNOWLEDGE OF CHURCH HISTORY (ANCIENT). *Edited by* JOHN HENRY BLUNT, M.A.

A KEY TO THE KNOWLEDGE OF CHURCH HISTORY (MODERN). *Edited by* JOHN HENRY BLUNT, M.A.

A KEY TO CHRISTIAN DOCTRINE AND PRACTICE. (*Founded on the Church Catechism.*) *By* JOHN HENRY BLUNT, M.A.

A KEY TO THE NARRATIVE OF THE FOUR GOSPELS. *By* JOHN PILKINGTON NORRIS, M.A., *Canon of Bristol, formerly one of Her Majesty's Inspectors of Schools.*

A KEY TO THE NARRATIVE OF THE ACTS OF THE APOSTLES. *By* JOHN PILKINGTON NORRIS, M.A.

Other Keys are in Preparation.

WATERLOO PLACE, PALL MALL, LONDON

New Publications.

Rivington's Mathematical Series.

12mo.

By **J. HAMBLIN SMITH, M.A.**, *of Gonville and Caius College, and late Lecturer at St. Peter's College, Cambridge.*

ALGEBRA. Part I. 2s. 6d.
With Answers, 3s.

EXERCISES ON ALGEBRA. Part I. 2s. 6d. Copies may be had without the Answers.

ELEMENTARY TRIGONOMETRY, 4s. 6d.

ELEMENTARY HYDROSTATICS. 3s.

ELEMENTS OF GEOMETRY. Containing the First Four Books of Euclid, with Exercises and Notes. 3s.
Books 1 and 2 } 2s. each; or limp
Books 3 and 4 } cloth, 1s. 6d.
The Concluding Part Nearly Ready.

ELEMENTARY STATICS. 3s.

By **E. J. GROSS, M.A.**, *Fellow of Gonville and Caius College, Cambridge.*

ALGEBRA. Part II.
[*In preparation.*

By **G. RICHARDSON, M.A.**, *Assistant Master at Winchester College, and late Fellow of St. John's College, Cambridge.*

GEOMETRICAL CONIC SECTIONS. [*In the Press.*

By **H. E. OAKELEY, M.A.**, *Late Fellow and Senior Mathematical Lecturer of Jesus College, Cambridge, H.M. Inspector of Schools.*

ANALYTICAL GEOMETRY OF TWO DIMENSIONS.
[*In preparation.*

Other Works are in Preparation.

AND AT OXFORD, AND CAMBRIDGE

Messrs. Rivington's

CATENA CLASSICORUM. *A Series of Classical Authors.* Edited by Members of both Universities, under the Direction of the REV. ARTHUR HOLMES, M.A., *Senior Fellow and Lecturer of Clare College, Cambridge, and Preacher at the Chapel Royal, Whitehall;* and the REV. CHARLES BIGG, M.A., *late Senior Student and Tutor of Christ Church, Oxford, Principal of Brighton College.*

SOPHOCLIS TRAGOEDIAE. Edited by R. C. JEBB, M.A., *Fellow and Assistant Tutor of Trinity College, Cambridge, and Public Orator of the University.*
THE ELECTRA. 3s. 6d.
THE AJAX. 3s. 6d.

JUVENALIS SATIRAE. Edited by G. A. SIMCOX, M.A., *Fellow and Classical Lecturer of Queen's College, Oxford.* 3s. 6d.

THUCYDIDIS HISTORIA. Edited by CHAS. BIGG, M.A., *late Senior Student and Tutor of Christ Church, Oxford; Principal of Brighton College.*
Books I. and II. with Introductions. 6s.

DEMOSTHENIS ORATIONES PUBLICAE. Edited by G. H. HESLOP, M.A., *late Fellow and Assistant Tutor of Queen's Col., Oxford; Head Master of St. Bees.*
THE OLYNTHIACS. 2s. 6d.
THE PHILIPPICS. 3s.
DE FALSA LEGATIONE. 6s.

ARISTOPHANIS COMOEDIAE. Edited by W. C. GREEN, M.A., *ate Fellow of King's College, Cambridge; Assistant Master at Rugby School.*
THE ACHARNIANS AND THE KNIGHTS. 4s.

THE CLOUDS. 3s. 6d.
THE WASPS. 3s. 6d.
An Edition of THE ACHARNIANS and THE KNIGHTS, Revised and especially adapted for Use in Schools. 4s.

ISOCRATIS ORATIONES. Edited by JOHN EDWIN SANDYS, M.A., *Fellow and Tutor of St. John's College, Classical Lecturer at Jesus College, Cambridge.*
AD DEMONICUM ET PANEGYRICUS. 4s. 6d.

PERSII SATIRAE. Edited by A. PRETOR, M.A., *of Trinity College, Cambridge, Classical Lecturer of Trinity Hall.* 3s. 6d.

HOMERI ILIAS. Edited by S. H. REYNOLDS, M.A., *Fellow and Tutor of Brasenose College, Oxford.*
Books I. to XII. 6s.

TERENTI COMOEDIAE. Edited by T. L. PAPILLON, M.A., *Fellow of New College, Oxford, late Fellow of Merton.*
ANDRIA ET EUNUCHUS. 4s. 6d.

DEMOSTHENIS ORATIONES PRIVATAE. Edited by the REV. ARTHUR HOLMES, M.A., *Senior Fellow and Lecturer of Clare College, Cambridge, and Preacher at the Chapel Royal, Whitehall.*
DE CORONA. 5s.

WATERLOO PLACE, PALL MALL, LONDON

New Publications.

DEVOTIONAL COMMENTARY ON THE GOSPEL NARRATIVE.
By the REV. ISAAC WILLIAMS, B.D., formerly Fellow of Trinity College, Oxford.

New Edition. Eight Volumes. Crown 8vo. 5s. each.

Thoughts on the Study of the Holy Gospels.
Characteristic Differences in the Four Gospels—Our Lord's Manifestations of Himself — The Rule of Scriptural Interpretation furnished by Our Lord—Analogies of the Gospel—Mention of Angels in the Gospels—Places of Our Lord's Abode and Ministry—Our Lord's Mode of Dealing with His Apostles—Conclusion.

A Harmony of the Four Evangelists.
Our Lord's Nativity—Our Lord's Ministry (Second Year)—Our Lord's Ministry (Third Year)—The Holy Week—Our Lord's Resurrection.

Our Lord's Nativity.
The Birth at Bethlehem—The Baptism in Jordan—The First Passover.

Our Lord's Ministry. Second Year.
The Second Passover—Christ with the Twelve—The Twelve sent Forth.

Our Lord's Ministry. Third Year.
Teaching in Galilee—Teaching at Jerusalem—Last Journey from Galilee to Jerusalem.

The Holy Week.
The Approach to Jerusalem—The Teaching in the Temple—The Discourse on the Mount of Olives—The Last Supper.

Our Lord's Passion.
The Hour of Darkness—The Agony—The Apprehension—The Condemnation—The Day of Sorrows—The Hall of Judgment—The Crucifixion—The Sepulture.

Our Lord's Resurrection.
The Day of Days—The Grave Visited—Christ Appearing—The Going to Emmaus—The Forty Days—The Apostles Assembled—The Lake in Galilee—The Mountain in Galilee—The Return from Galilee.

AND AT OXFORD, AND CAMBRIDGE

Rivington's Devotional Series.

Elegantly printed with red borders. 16mo. 2s. 6d.

THOMAS À KEMPIS, OF THE IMITATION OF CHRIST.

THE RULE AND EXERCISES OF HOLY LIVING. *By* JEREMY TAYLOR, D.D., *Bishop of Down and Connor, and Dromore.*

INTRODUCTION TO THE DEVOUT LIFE. *From the French of S. Francis of Sales, Bishop and Prince of Geneva.*

THE RULE AND EXERCISES OF HOLY DYING. *By* JEREMY TAYLOR, D.D., *Bishop of Down and Connor, and Dromore.*

The "HOLY LIVING" and the "HOLY DYING" may be had bound together in One Vol., 5s.

A SHORT AND PLAIN INSTRUCTION FOR THE BETTER UNDERSTANDING OF THE LORD'S SUPPER; *to which is annexed, the Office of the Holy Communion, with proper Helps and Directions.* By THOMAS WILSON, D.D., *late Lord Bishop of Sodor and Man.*
Complete Edition, in large type.

A PRACTICAL TRATISE CONCERNING EVIL THOUGHTS. *By* WILLIAM CHILCOT, M.A.

THE ENGLISH POEMS OF GEORGE HERBERT. *Together with his Collection of Proverbs, entitled "Jacula Prudentum."*

Cheap Editions, without the red borders.

THOMAS À KEMPIS, OF THE IMITATION OF CHRIST. Limp cloth, 1s.; or in cover, 6d.

BISHOP WILSON'S HOLY COMMUNION. Large type. Limp cloth, 1s.; or in cover, 6d.

JEREMY TAYLOR'S HOLY LIVING.
JEREMY TAYLOR'S HOLY DYING.
Limp cloth, 1s. each.

HOLY LIVING and HOLY DYING, in One Volume, 2s. 6d.

WATERLOO PLACE, PALL MALL, LONDON
HIGH STREET, OXFORD; and TRINITY STREET, CAMBRIDGE

www.ingramcontent.com/pod-product-compliance
Lightning Source LLC
Chambersburg PA
CBHW021802230426
43669CB00008B/608